A Celebration of
neurons

AN
EDUCATOR'S
GUIDE
TO THE
HUMAN BRAIN

ROBERT SYLWESTER

ASSOCIATION FOR SUPERVISION AND CURRICULUM DEVELOPMENT
ALEXANDRIA, VIRGINIA

Association for Supervision and Curriculum Development
1250 N. Pitt Street, Alexandria, VA 22314
Telephone (703) 549-9110, Fax (703) 549-3891

Ronald S. Brandt, *Director, Publications*
Nancy Modrak, *Managing Editor, ASCD Books*
Julie Houtz, *Senior Associate Editor*
Biz McMahon, *Assistant Editor*
Gary Bloom, *Manager, Design and Production Services*
Karen Monaco, *Senior Graphic Designer*
Stephanie Justen, *Print Production Coordinator*
Valerie Sprague, *Desktop Publisher*

Medical Illustrations by Lydia Kibiuk

ASCD Stock No.: 1-95085

From the Editors:
We welcome readers' comments on ASCD books and other publications. If you would like to give us your opinion of this book or suggest topics for future books, please write to ASCD, Managing Editor of Books, 1250 N. Pitt St., Alexandria, VA 22314.

Library of Congress Cataloging-in-Publication Data
Sylwester, Robert.
    A celebration of neurons : an educator's guide to the human brain
/ Robert Sylwester.
    p. cm.
    Includes bibliographical references and index.
    ISBN 0-87120-243-3
    1. Cognitive neuroscience.   I. Title.
QP360.5.S96 1995
612.8'2—dc20
                                                           95-4382
                                                             CIP

ABOUT THE AUTHOR

Robert Sylwester, Professor of Education at the University of Oregon, focuses on the educational applications of new developments in brain/stress theory and research. He has written dozens of journal articles and made hundreds of conference and inservice presentations.

You can reach him at the College of Education, University of Oregon, Eugene, Oregon 97403-1215. Phone: (503) 345-1452. Fax: (503) 346-5174.

A CELEBRATION OF NEURONS
AN EDUCATOR'S GUIDE
TO THE HUMAN BRAIN

FOREWORD

In this intriguing and timely book, Robert Sylwester provides an important introduction to the current scientific understanding of our brain and its processes. *A Celebration of Neurons* will do much to remedy educators' fragmented understanding of developments in the cognitive sciences. Its relatively simple descriptions, concrete examples, and clear illustrations make a complex subject accessible to even the most uninformed reader.

I found Chapter 4, "How Our Brain Determines What's Important," particularly compelling. Here, Sylwester explores the importance of emotion in the educational process and outlines a half dozen themes that have emerged from the emotion research, including the effects of stress on our ability to learn and the importance of emotional context in the formation of memories. From the research, we can see that emotions are hard-wired into our being; they cannot be separated out. When we try to eliminate them from our classrooms, we work against our brain's own intelligence. "John Dewey began this century," Sylwester writes, "with an eloquent plea for the education of the whole child. It would be good for us to get around to it by the end of the century—and emotion research may well be the catalyst we need."

The role of emotions in learning is but one example of the serious issues that will sooner or later come under discussion as the results of recent brain research become more widely known. If we are serious about educating all our students, then I think we must take Sylwester's lead and educate ourselves about the development, organization, and operation of the brain. We have a lot of catching up to do. The scientific discoveries will continue regardless of our response, but the loss could be great if we do not actively seek to learn about and use brain research to improve teaching and learning in our schools. I hope you take the first step and use what you learn from this book to explore new ways of interacting with students.

— CHARLES E. PATTERSON
ASCD President, 1995–96

PREFACE

Recent dramatic developments in the cognitive sciences are moving us closer to an understanding of our brain's development, organization, and operation. Increased understanding of the brain should lead to widespread discussions of the important issues that will arise out of these advances, and to the development of appropriate and effective educational applications of this knowledge.

As an educational leader, you need a functional understanding of these significant developments to be able to comprehend the growing scientific and professional writing in this field; discuss, develop, and evaluate proposed educational applications; and effectively teach students about brain mechanisms and processes. Without such knowledge, our profession will become prey for educational hucksters who will propose expensive programs they claim to be compatible with current cognitive theory and research.

This nontechnical book provides a functional introduction to that professionally important information. It's directed especially to educational leaders who have a limited background in the cognitive sciences, but who will be expected to make the educational decisions sparked by developments in the scientific world. It's an introduction to our brain, not a comprehensive treatment. You'll need to read much more to become truly informed, so the text and especially the chapter notes recommend excellent nontechnical books and articles written by respected scientists and science writers who have the ability to explain complex biochemical processes in layman's terms. Your continued study will spark imaginative thoughts that will lead to new ways of looking at your profession, to the design of biologically based educational applications, to the excitement of curricular experimentation.

The book's title, *A Celebration of Neurons*, uses the poetic collective noun *celebration* (as in a *pride* of lions, a *swarm* of bees) to communicate the celebratory nature of the magnificent network of neurons we humans have. It's the only mass of matter in the known universe that can contemplate itself—a true celebration of neurons.

The book begins with the cognitive sciences' recent and rapid rise to importance in educational thought and practice. Subsequent chapters examine specific educationally significant elements of our brain and its processes. Although the book focuses on our current scientific understanding of our brain and its processes, it also suggests some broad educational applications—all based on current theory and research—that can be introduced in schools now.

The suggested applications probably won't surprise you because the cognitive sciences are discovering all sorts of things that good teachers have always intuitively known. What's important, however, is that our profession is now getting strong scientific support for many practices that our critics have decried.

Our profession is at the edge of a major transformation. The scientific discoveries will continue at an increasing pace whether or not we inform ourselves and make the effort to discover appropriate educational applications. What a tragedy it would be, though, if we were to choose to remain professionally uninformed and uninvolved in this historic revolution.

This book had its beginnings in 20 syntheses of cognitive science theory and research that I've published over the past 15 years, many in *Educational Leadership*. I'm grateful to Ron Brandt of ASCD for his constant support in this enterprise, and to the Education Press Association of America for the four encouraging awards they've given my published syntheses. The cognitive sciences are developing so rapidly, however, that I practically had to start from scratch in writing this book.

I'm especially appreciative of my wife Ruth's constant unconditional support—and since I've come to understand cognitive development in ways that I couldn't have imagined when our own children were young, I'm thankful for the second chance our children have provided us to observe its development in our dozen grandchildren.

— ROBERT SYLWESTER

1

AT THE EDGE

OF A MAJOR

TRANSFORMATION

The human brain is the best organized, most functional three pounds of matter in the known universe. It's responsible for Beethoven's Ninth Symphony, computers, the Sistine Chapel, automobiles, the Second World War, Hamlet, apple pie, and a whole lot more. Our brain has always defined the education profession, yet educators haven't really understood it or paid much attention to it.

For a long time, scientists didn't understand the brain either. Our skull hides a bewildering array of electrochemical activity, so our brain's awesome complexity is its own major barrier to understanding itself. Our brain's cellular units are tiny, their numbers are immense, and everything is connected.

At the cellular level, our brain's three-pint, three-pound mass is divided somewhat evenly between tens of billions of nerve cells, or neurons, that regulate cognitive activity, and the much smaller and ten-times-more-numerous glial cells that support, insulate, and nourish the neurons.

Brain cells are very small and highly interconnected. Thirty thousand neurons (or 300,000 glial cells) can fit into a space the size of a pinhead. Neurons connect to other neurons, muscles, or glands via sending and receiving extensions; and although most sending connections are in the millimeter range, the extensions connecting some motor neurons to muscles can reach a meter in length. A neuron may connect to thousands of other cells, so the chemical information in a neuron is only a few neurons away from any other neuron. If you think that's implausible, consider our world's one billion telephones—and the relatively simple coding system of about a dozen digits that can rapidly connect any two of them.

Enter into a single neuron and the complexity increases. For example, a cell's nucleus contains DNA (deoxyribonucleic acid), a relatively large molecule that is the cell's recipe book for manufacturing cellular materials and regulating cellular processes. In human neurons, the unraveled ladder-shaped DNA molecule is a meter long—in a cell 1/30,000 the size of a pinhead!

Pioneer brain researchers obviously had problems when they tried to study individual neurons or interconnected assemblies of neurons. They simply didn't have the technology for such investigation, and so their research progress was slow and tentative. Still, these researchers had the freedom to patiently explore what they could of the brain, and to slowly develop more sophisticated chemical assay and monitoring technology to study the remainder. This technology has evolved rapidly during the current computer age, as have the research fields that study the brain—with greater wonders yet to come. Our brain is at the edge of understanding itself!

A Behaviorist Profession

Educators have never had the scientist's freedom to patiently wait for the research technology to catch up with their curiosity. Every year, a new batch of students arrives at the school door, whether we understand how their brains develop or not. We have had to find a way to bypass students' brains in order to carry out our professional assignment.

Our solution has been to focus on the visible, measurable, pliable manifestations of cognition, rather than on cognitive mechanisms and processes. The human brain uses sensory/perceptual processes to take in objects and events in the environment. It then draws on memory and various problem-solving strategies to process the information, and it eventually translates thought and decision into behavior. If our profession couldn't comprehend internal brain processes, it could focus on knowable external objects or events in the environment (stimulus) and the behavior (response) that emerged out of the unknowable cognitive processes. Thus, we became a profession of behaviorists, whether we liked it or not. We learned how to manipulate the student's environment to achieve the behavior we desired.

We didn't do all that badly with this approach. Millions of intelligent and sharing teachers, each observing the behavior of about thirty students for a thousand hours every year, eventually learned many practical and effective things about teaching and learning. When the findings of formal educational and psychological research were added to this experience, our informal knowledge evolved into a solid base of normative, practical professional knowledge.

To be honest, though, the practical base of our profession was probably closer to folklore knowledge than scientific knowledge. We could predict what would probably occur in a classroom, but we generally didn't know why it occurred. For example, we knew that more boys than girls had serious reading problems, and that hyperactive students tended to be thin, blond, blue-eyed boys, but we didn't know why. The problem with partial knowledge that focuses only on outward behavior is that it can lead to inappropriate, generalized conclusions, such as that boys are inherently stupid and ill-mannered.

We also didn't understand the underlying mechanisms that govern other significant teaching and learning concerns, such as emotion, interest, attention, thinking, memory, and skill development—even though we did learn how to deal with the outward behavior. Thus, studying student behavior was professionally useful, but we knew intuitively that behavior was only part of a much larger picture. Deep down, we could never be sure if students learned because of our efforts, or despite them. We accepted this blind spot as a limitation of our profession.

Perhaps a more serious issue is that the study of behavior can lead us to only a partial diagnosis and treatment of many complex learning behaviors that we've handled rather ineffectively. These include dyslexia, attention disorders, motivation, and forgetting. Schools tend to be most successful with motivated students of at least average ability who come from secure homes and can function reasonably well without much teacher assistance. They are less successful with students who don't fit this profile.

A Medical Analogy

The medical profession, too, operated at the level of professional folklore for most of its long history. Doctors weren't very effective at treating health problems that were much more serious than those the body's own recuperative powers could heal with time and rest. The romantic vision of the pioneer family doctor is of a caring and sometimes helpful person who could correctly diagnose an illness, but only sit helpless at the bedside as the patient died. Worse, earlier well-meaning doctors actually hastened their patients' deaths because they didn't realize that doctors should wash their hands and sterilize their instruments before treating a patient.

As medical knowledge improved, doctors reached the point where they could explain the cause of an illness to a patient, but still not be able to offer a cure. Later they discovered a cure, but it didn't always work. Finally, they could nearly always successfully treat the illness that had resulted in almost certain death a few decades earlier.

The medical profession's move from the careful but often ineffectual observation of the patient's body and behavior to the successful diagnosis and treatment of complex health problems began when it developed sound theories and the research skills and technologies needed to study the structure and biochemistry of the body and its organs.

If the medical profession had waited for the cure to suddenly appear before it did anything about understanding the illness, patients would still be waiting for miracle cures. Each stage of the progression of diagnosis and treatment, including the errors made along the way, was legitimate for its time and necessary for our advancement to the next stage.

Our Professional Challenge

The education profession is now approaching a crossroads. We can continue to focus our energies on the careful observation of external behavior—a course that may be adequate for managing relatively mild learning disorders—or we can join the search for a scientific understanding of the brain mechanisms, processes, and malfunctions that affect the successful completion of complex learning tasks.

Getting involved in the exciting developments in the brain sciences is an important step for educators, even though the educational applications of much of this research aren't yet clear (e.g., to know why language and attention problems are more prevalent in boys than girls doesn't really solve the problem of how to teach students). Understanding brain mechanisms and processes adds an exciting dimension to our thoughts about our profession. Few things fascinate us more than our own cognitive processes.

It's true that you don't have to know how an internal combustion engine is put together in order to drive a car, but you ought to have a functional understanding of the engine if you're going to sell cars, and you must have a technical understanding of it if you're going to repair cars. By analogy, the education profession will have to decide if its knowledge of the human brain ought to be closer to the level of those who merely use their brain, those who give advice on how best to use it, or those who repair malfunctions of the brain. Only through our knowledge of the research and our profession's own experimental fumblings will we begin to discover useful applications of brain theory and research. *Knowing why* generally leads to *knowing how to.*

Many educators lack the natural science background to understand cognitive science research, let alone to participate in it, or to create a curriculum around it. Because our profession's orientation has long been in the social and behavioral sciences, teacher education students rarely do much academic work in biology, chemistry, and cognitive psychology. This preservice focus was perhaps appropriate within the traditional view that classroom teaching focuses on negotiated activity in a group setting. The educationally significant new developments in brain theory and research suggest,

5

however, that the amount of natural science in our professional preparation must increase—at both the preservice and inservice levels.

Can a profession whose charge is defined by the development of an effective and efficient human brain continue to remain uninformed about that brain? If we do remain uninformed, we will become vulnerable to the pseudoscientific fads, generalizations, and programs that will surely arise from the pool of brain research. We've already demonstrated our vulnerability with the educational spillover of the split-brain research: the right brain/left brain books, workshops, and curricular programs whose recommendations often went far beyond the research findings. If we can't offer informed leadership on the complex educational issues arising from current brain theory and research, we can expect that other people—perhaps just as uninformed as we are—will soon make decisions for us.

Our profession is at the edge of a major transformation. We can expect a marked increase in scientific knowledge about our brain and its processes. We can expect a similar increase in our patrons' awareness of such developments, because the mass media generally report and discuss such developments. Think about what we knew about our brain 20 years ago and compare it with what we know today; then project our current level of understanding 20 years into the future, when today's kindergarten student might be a beginning teacher.

Imagine the shape of our nation's health if the medical profession had, by default, been content to remain at the level of folklore and home remedies when it was at a similar point of decision.[1]

How Our Brain Studies Itself

Our brain has long contemplated itself, and it is rapidly moving toward understanding itself. This chapter began with the suggestion that our brain is awesomely complex, but our brain is also elegantly simple. Let's turn now to the search for that elegant simplicity.

The Scientists Who Study the Brain

The scientists who study brain mechanisms and processes approach their task from one of two general directions: from the bottom up or from the top down.

In studying our brain from the bottom up, the researcher focuses on the workings of small units—individual cells, or small systems of cells within more complex systems. This research perspective argues that understanding the basic units of a system is essential to understanding the entire system. Scientists who study brains from the bottom up are generally called neuroscientists, and many of them specialize in the study of a single cellular brain mechanism or process. Neuroscience has become a major research field during the past 25 years because researchers have developed the technology needed to study the brain's tiny and highly interconnected cells.

Studying our brain from the top down means that the researcher/scholar focuses on complex cognitive mechanisms, functions, or behaviors, such as movement, language, and abstract analysis. Cognitive psychology, linguistics, physical anthropology, philosophy, and artificial intelligence are some of the fields that use this broader approach. The top-down approach to brain study developed before the bottom-up approach because it was initially more tolerant of logical inference and speculations that weren't strongly supported by experimental evidence. Without the research technology to monitor cellular activity, top-down researchers/scholars had to infer brain activity from external behavior and brain malfunctions.

Because a brain is such a complex organ, most brain researchers/scholars focus their study at one level. Klivington (1986) uses a computer analogy to suggest three legitimate levels for understanding the development and operation of complex systems. In his analogy, the top level is software, and understanding a computer at this level means knowing how to write computer programs. The intermediate level is logic circuitry, the electrical hardware of information processing; understanding a computer at this level means knowing how to design logic circuitry and computer hardware. The bottom level is the solid-state physics of semiconductors in the component transistors, and a good background in physics is crucial to understanding the computer at this level.

7

This analogy suggests that a computer programmer, a circuit designer, and a solid-state physicist can each claim to know how a computer works without knowing much of what the other two specialists know. Similarly, a philosopher, a psychologist, and a neuroscientist all understand how a brain works, but at three different levels of understanding (one is reminded of John Saxe's 19th century poem of the six blind men and the elephant, each defining the elephant on the basis of his limited tactile exploration of it).

We thus have an organ and its functions that can be studied and understood at multiple levels. But it's difficult to know at what level something like conscious thought emerges from the movement of molecules within our brain. Think of the two atoms of hydrogen and one atom of oxygen that make up a water molecule, and then ask yourself how many molecules you would have to combine to achieve wetness, an important property of water. The abstract concept of consciousness is perhaps similar to wetness, in that it emerges in the system only when enough related molecular activity occurs in relevant neural networks. But at this point, scientists don't know for sure how much molecular activity in our brain is enough to create conscious thought, or where it occurs.

How Scientists Study a Brain

If our brain's awesome complexity hindered neuroscience research, its elegantly simplicity enhanced it. A human brain has to be simple, adaptable, and predictable to function continuously for upwards of a hundred years. To learn more about the brain, scientists had to discover how to perform intricate studies that would provide solid information on our brain's most basic operations: the normal and abnormal actions of a single neuron, the synchronized actions of networks of neurons, and the factors that trigger neuronal activity.

Thus, scientists developed laboratory procedures and brain-monitoring technology that could (1) collect electrochemical data from individual neurons and widespread neural networks, (2) summarize and interpret the relevant data and ignore the rest, and (3) graphically report neural activity in a form that researchers/scholars could understand. This search for useful information led scientists to study the brains and behaviors of animals with simple neural systems. They also studied people and primates with and without brain damage or mental illness, and developed brain-imaging technologies that could take them beyond observable behavior.

Animal Research. Our brain's complexity and general inaccessibility limit its direct use in the study of basic neural functions. Fortunately, basic neural mechanisms and processes are similar in all animals, so neuroscientists searched for animals with simple nervous systems that would be relatively easy to study with the microelectrodes they had developed to record the activity of single neurons. Some of the invertebrates proved especially useful, because they have only a few thousand neurons that are all much larger than human neurons. Invertebrates also have a limited behavioral repertoire and simple neural networks that are identical in all animals in the species. The marine snails *Aplysia* and *Hermissenda* have proved especially useful in this research, providing much of our knowledge about changes that occur in connecting neurons during learning and memory formation.[2]

Neuroscientists have also used a wide variety of other animals, such as squid, rats, cats, rabbits, and monkeys, that have brain mechanisms especially suited to a specific research problem. For example, major discoveries emerged when researchers used rabbits to study the role of the cerebellum in procedural memory processes, cats to study the structure of the visual cortex, and rats to study the effect of the environment on brain development.

The animal rights movement is critical of the use of animals in such research. Animal studies, however, have provided most of what we know about basic brain mechanisms and processes. This information has helped improve the lives of both humans and animals (albeit not the animals used in the research), and brain researchers argue that they currently have no other avenue to this kind of information. Animal rights activists argue that a perceived human need doesn't morally justify the killing of animals. So it's a real social dilemma. Each side argues its case persuasively, and the issue doesn't lend itself to simple compromise.

People with Brain Damage or Mental Illness. The dramatic bottom-up discoveries of cellular changes that occur during learning in a marine snail didn't directly help us to understand how children learn the multiplication tables. Although the individual neurons of snails and humans are remarkably similar, a snail's

9

nervous system isn't similar to a human brain. Thus, researchers with a top-down interest in brain mechanisms and processes needed to discover a research approach that would allow them to study our brain directly, in all its complexity.

The obvious experimental limitations they faced forced them to focus their studies on available research subjects, generally people with brain damage or mental illness. War and accident injuries suffered by otherwise healthy young people provide the best subjects for this kind of research. People with such problems tend to allow researchers to study them in the hope that the discoveries will improve their plight.

The basic research design is straightforward: (1) identify the nature and general location of the subject's brain malfunction, (2) compare the subject's behavior to that of people without brain damage, in an attempt to link any abnormal behavior to the malfunctioning section of the brain, and (3) if possible, do a postmortem examination of the subject's brain to test the inference.

This approach has research design problems. The unpredictable availability of subjects permits researchers to only rarely conduct the controlled experiments critical to scientific research. Further, it's difficult to precisely locate a specific function in our brain because neurons are synaptically connected to thousands of other neurons in very complex, interacting networks. Still, researchers using this approach made some remarkable discoveries, although they often waited years to get enough subjects with the same problem to adequately study a function (or malfunction). Educators today are perhaps most acquainted with Roger Sperry's split-brain research (for which he won a 1981 Nobel Prize). The learning styles movement and many right-brain/left-brain books and workshops emerged from this research.

The split-brain research on humans had its beginnings in related research on the two hemispheres of cat brains. The two cerebral hemispheres that make up most of the mass of our brain are connected by the *corpus callosum*, a large group of neural fibers that allow the two hemispheres to communicate with each other and to collaborate on many complex cognitive functions. The success of the cat research encouraged doctors to cut the corpus callosum of patients suffering almost continuous epileptic seizures, in the hope that this radical surgical procedure would reduce the effects of the seizures. The procedure was effective in that it reduced the seizures, and it didn't seem to negatively affect the patient's mental or emotional life.

Brain researchers saw the split-brain patients as a rich source of valuable experimental data. The severed corpus callosum left each with practically no communication between the brain hemispheres, so for the first time in the history of brain research, scientists had an opportunity to discover the hemispheric location of specific cognitive processes.

The two hemispheres divide the visual information coming into each eye. The information from the left side of the visual field is sent to the right hemisphere, and vice versa. The researchers developed imaginative techniques that allowed them to send visual information into one hemisphere while blocking the information that would go into the other hemisphere. By asking probing questions and observing the subject's behaviors, the researchers believed they could discover which brain hemisphere normally processes specific cognitive functions. They also created related tests for hearing and touch.

Over the years, several dozen people with split brains have been extensively studied in increasingly sophisticated tests, and much of our early understanding of the division of cognitive functions between the hemispheres came from the study of these subjects.[3] The literature on learning and memory often discusses an interesting case that came out of this type of research. The unfortunate man is known as H.M., and his story is another example of one person's tragedy resulting in a major increase in our understanding of an important brain mechanism.

In 1953, a surgeon removed the entire hippocampus of H.M. in a radical attempt to treat his epilepsy (the hippocampus is a wishbone-shaped structure that straddles the brainstem). The procedure has never been repeated, but it left H.M. with a permanent inability to form new factual memories, although he can remember things that occurred before his operation. He can hold information in his short-term memory for up to ten minutes, but he can't transfer it into long-term memory. For example, he has to be reintroduced to people who have left the room for 15 minutes or so. He has been extensively studied since the operation, and much that we know about the important role the hippocampus plays in long-term memory formation comes from studies of H.M.

Laboratory Experiments with Normal Primates and Humans. As cognitive scientists have learned more about our brain, they've developed increasingly sophisticated laboratory studies that allow them to study specific brain functions in normal humans and primates. For example, by carefully observing eye movements during the execution of a task, they can infer how the brain processes various spatial elements in our environment, and by timing response rates, they can determine how a brain processes various temporal elements, such as sequences.

The Stroop Test is an interesting example of the imaginative tests that cognitive scientists have developed—in this case to discover how rapidly and effectively our brain responds to conflicting information. The researcher asks the subject to read aloud a list of color names that are printed in a different color (e.g., the word *red* is printed in *blue* ink) or to say the color the word is printed in rather than the word itself.

Brain-Imaging Technology. As productive as these early studies were, it was obvious that brain researchers would eventually have to develop technologies and procedures that could directly represent (image) the activity of a normal, active human brain. The rapid development of computer technology during the past two decades made brain-imaging machines possible and revolutionized brain research.

Brain-imaging machines gather and rapidly process the vast amounts of electrochemical data continuously generated by our brain, and so take researchers well beyond observable behavior, two-dimensional black-and-white x-rays, and EEG reports—and into the world of three-dimensional color TV graphics with high spatial and temporal resolution. Imaging machines can now focus to within one millimeter of a specific slice of brain tissue, much as an optical camera can focus on a specific plane in the photographed scene. Using imaging machines, researchers need only a few hours to gather from the brain the same type of data that formerly took 20 years of inferential laboratory work with nonhuman primates (Blakeslee 1993). New technological wonders and brain properties to explore will continue to emerge in this field.[4]

The current brain-imaging technology focuses on three elements of the organization and operation of our brain: (1) the chemical composition of cells and neurotransmitters, (2) the electrical transmission of information along neuronal fibers and the magnetic fields that brain activity generates, and (3) the distribution of blood through the brain as it replenishes energy used in electrochemical activity.

Chemical Composition. The CAT scan (short for computerized axial tomography) and MRI (magnetic resonance imaging) are examples of technologies that create graphic, even three-dimensional, images of the anatomical structures of our body/brain, thus locating features and malfunctions. The CAT scan uses multiple x-rays to provide the depth-of-field and clear cross-sectional views of features that simple x-rays don't provide. These multiple x-rays respond to the density of the tissue being scanned, showing dark shadows for denser elements, such as bones or tumors, and various shades of gray for the soft tissue that constitutes our brain. The MRI, with its focus on soft tissue, provides the reverse image. It responds to chemical differences in the composition of various brain and body tissues (while ignoring bones, moving blood, etc.), and thus it provides a clear image of the chemical composition of our brain. Fast MRI is a remarkable new development that allows researchers to observe brain activity on a TV monitor while the subject is carrying out a cognitive action.

Electrical Transmission. The EEG (electroencephalogram) has been in use for over half a century, reporting patterns in the electrical transmission of information within an active brain. Translating a score of squiggly lines on a moving sheet of paper into an accurate vision of brain activity is difficult, however, and the convolutions in the cerebral cortex make it difficult to pinpoint the exact source of the electrical activity. The SQUID (superconducting quantum interference device) is a major advance in this technology that uses the more easily located small magnetic fields produced by the brain. The BEAM machine (brain electrical activity mapping) represents another major advance in this technology. It records the electrical activity from more precisely defined areas and then uses color gradations to represent positive and negative levels in the analogous location on a TV screen's easily interpreted graphic representation of the cerebral cortex.

Blood Flow Patterns. PET (positron emission tomography) uses radioactive materials to monitor the unequally distributed patterns of the pint and a half of blood that flows through our brain every minute. It thus traces sequential changes in brain energy use as various parts of our brain are activated. PET research has provided some recent dramatic advances in our knowledge of how and where our brain processes a series of events.

Brain-imaging machines are expensive, so their use thus far has been limited to medical research and diagnosis facilities and university science and psychology departments. Computer technology tends to become cheaper and more powerful over time, however. Researchers in university education departments have just begun to use electrical imaging technologies, and we can expect this use to increase in the years ahead, as the technology advances. Eventually, K–12 schools will probably use adaptations of these technologies in the diagnosis and treatment of learning problems, as the graduate students involved in such university research move into jobs in school districts.

The use of this technology in schools would certainly mark another giant step over the professional folklore line, but with it will come many of the problems the medical profession faced after it crossed that line: increased expectations from patrons, new ethical issues, and the threat of malpractice suits.

But then, we can't really go back either. We will have to adapt our profession to the inevitable increase in our understanding of the brain mechanisms and processes that define our profession.

New Brain Hypotheses and Theories

Successful research requires a strong theoretic base that explains the relationships among the various elements in a researched phenomenon. In the past few years, the cognitive sciences have seen a flurry of activity in the development of theories that use biological processes to explain complex cognitive functions—theories that scientists can test using the research technologies described earlier. This theoretical work, along with developments in genetics, may spark a Century of Biology, just as Albert Einstein's theories sparked advances in physics that have dominated the 20th century.

The new biologically based brain theories focus on the developmental relationship between a brain's ancestors and its current environment: the "nature versus nurture" issue. Our profession has tended to think of the *nurture* side as dominant, but these new theories argue that *nature* plays a far more important role than previously believed—or that the dichotomy itself is now an irrelevant issue. They also suggest that many current beliefs about instruction, learning, and memory are wrong. These theories will become controversial because they will require reconceptualizations of such concepts as parenting, teaching, learning, intelligence, identity, free will, and human potential. Further, some people may misuse the theories to support racist, sexist, and elitist beliefs. Certainly, those who reject Darwinian evolution will be disturbed by the evolutionary base of the new theories.

When these brain theories and their strong supporting evidence shortly reach the awareness of the general public, educational leaders will be asked to comment on them. The thrust of these theories raises fundamental issues about our professional assignment, so we had better understand them.

This discussion will focus on the work of two Nobel laureates whose work in brain theory has attracted much attention in the scientific community—and will probably attract much controversy as it moves into the educational community and general public awareness.

Francis Crick: The Astonishing Hypothesis

Francis Crick and James Watson collaborated in the 1953 discovery of the molecular structure of DNA, a form of memory that passes from one generation to the next genetic information about how to construct and maintain a body (Crick, Watson, and Maurice H. F. Wilkins received a Nobel Prize in 1962 for their work with DNA). Crick subsequently joined the staff of the Salk Institute for Biological Studies, where he shifted his focus to understanding such things as the memories that a brain processes in its lifetime. He was especially interested in the related issues of consciousness and free will—how and where we are aware of what we know and what we do. He felt that consciousness would have to be an essential element of any global brain theory. Thus, in his scientific career he has moved from identifying the DNA molecule in our cells that directs life to identifying the networks of cells in our brain that give conscious meaning to life.

What has emerged from Crick's work is not a theory, but a hypothesis that he hopes will guide scientists in the development of sound brain theories that will spark further research. Crick has published his work in a fascinating but controversial book for general readers who have an interest in the cognitive sciences, *The Astonishing Hypothesis: The Scientific Search for the Soul* (Crick 1994). His astonishing hypothesis is that *everything* that constitutes who each of us is as a human being involves nothing more than the behavior of a vast assembly of nerve cells and their related molecules. *Everything* includes all of our interior states—our joys and sorrows, memories and ambitions, our loves and hatreds, our sense of personal identity and free will. It's an astonishing hypothesis because it goes against the feeling that many, if not most, people have: that we're certainly more than a pack of functioning neurons, that we also have a *disembodied* mind, spirit, self. And it certainly goes against many religious beliefs.

Crick used this hypothesis to guide his biological search for the soul (or consciousness) within neural networks. He focused his initial efforts on our visual system, the window to our soul. It's the brain system that scientists understand best, and Crick believes that if scientists can identify the neural systems that collaborate to create visual awareness (or consciousness), they can then move on to other cognitive processes, such as hearing and touch, in the development of a global, biologically based theory of consciousness.

Over the course of his book, Crick proposes what he considers to be a plausible model of the visual system that could explain visual awareness—how and where our brain *knows* (and attends to) what it sees. The thalamus, in the center of our brain, appears to play an especially important role. It's the relay center between our sense organs and the cortex, the large, folded sheet of neurons on the top of our brain that processes and remembers the objects and events we experience. Innate and learned biases toward certain kinds of visual information, and reverberating circuits between the thalamus and cortex, help to identify the important elements in the current visual field and to activate a synchronized firing pattern among the various networks that process the elements. This process holds the important information within our attentional and short-term memory systems, ignores the less important information, and thus seems to create the visual awareness we experience.

Suppose that I've gone to the airport to meet someone. I know what flight he's on and that he's a 40-year-old man who is six feet tall and will be wearing glasses and a red sweater. This descriptive information will focus my attentional mechanisms to those properties, and I'll attend only to incoming passengers who fit at least some of them. What occurs in my brain is thus a mix of (1) my direct perception of the man himself and (2) internal cognitive processes that prime certain networks to fire more easily than they normally would in a crowd of strangers.

Gerald Edelman: The Theory of Neuronal Group Selection

Gerald Edelman shared with Rodney Porter the 1972 Nobel Prize in physiology or medicine for a major discovery about how our immune system operates. Like Francis Crick, he then turned his attention to our brain. He is currently the Director of the Neuroscience Institute and Chairman of the Department of Neurobiology at the Scripps Research Institute.

Edelman's move from our immune system to the brain isn't as strange as it may seem. Our immune system is a sort of loose brain, in that most immune cells float free in our body, while our brain's neurons function within a highly interconnected web. Both systems are functionally similar, however, for both are highly integrated systems that recognize and respond to a wide variety of potentially helpful and hurtful stimuli. From the sensory information that reaches our skin's surface, our brain creates an internal mental model of external objects and events, and then responds appropriately to friend and foe. Our immune system examines the shapes of antigens that invade our body, and then destroys those that pose dangers to our body.

Edelman won the Nobel Prize for his discovery that the immune system doesn't operate through an instruction/memory model, as had been thought, but rather through evolutionary natural-selection procedures. The earlier belief was that generic antibody cells *learned* to recognize harmful antigen invaders, such as bacteria and viruses. The immune system then destroyed the antigens, and the system *remembered* the shape of the invader in the event of subsequent invasions. Edelman, however, found that through natural-selection processes occurring over eons of time, we are born with a vast number of specific antibodies, each of which recognizes and responds to a specific type of harmful invader that shares our environment. If we lack such a natural immunity to a specific invader (such as the AIDS virus), we may die if infected. Our immune system can't *learn* how to destroy the invader; it simply has or hasn't the capacity at birth.

Edelman then studied our functionally similar brain to see if it also operates principally on natural selection, rather than on instruction and learning. His controversial theory, the theory of neuronal group selection (or neural Darwinism, as it's more commonly called) argues that our brain does operate on the basis of natural selection—or at least that natural selection is the process that explains instruction and learning.

Edelman's theory currently appears to be the most completely developed biological brain theory, so the remainder of this chapter will focus on it. Edelman developed his theory through four books published since 1987. The latest, *Bright Air, Brilliant Fire* (Edelman 1992), presents the most complete and informal explanation of his complex theory, so it is the best resource for educators with a limited background in science (though it is challenging reading material).[5]

A New Brain Model. We tend to use simple models to help us understand complex phenomena, but the model we choose can sometimes hinder our understanding. The computer is the prevailing model of our brain, and an appealing one, but Edelman (along with other brain theorists) argues that it's an inappropriate model because a computer is developed, programmed, and run by an external force, and our brain isn't. (Terms such as teacher and parent come to mind as the *programmers* for our brain.) A computer model biases our thoughts toward filing and operating systems that differ significantly from the way our brain processes information. For example, most brain memories appear to be stored in the same locations that carry out current operations. Further, the powerful role that emotion plays in regulating brain activity, and the preponderance of parallel (rather than linear) processing in our brain, suggest to Edelman that a useful model for our brain must come out of biology, not technology.

Edelman suggests a better model: that the electrochemical dynamics of our brain's development and operation resemble the rich, layered ecology of a jungle environment. A jungle has no external developer, no predetermined goals. Indeed, it's a messy place characterized more by organic excess than by goal-directed economy and efficiency. No one organism or group runs the jungle. All plants and animals participate in the process, each carrying out a variety of ecological functions. A tree is a single organism, but it also participates in many symbiotic activities with other organisms (e.g., insects, birds, vines, and moss). It doesn't develop its limbs as a nesting site for birds, but birds use the limbs for that purpose.

Further, the jungle environment doesn't instruct organisms how to behave in an ecologically appropriate manner, for example, by teaching trees how to position their limbs and roots to get sunlight and soil nutrients. It's more a matter of natural selection, in an evolutionary sense. All trees have the innate capacity to reach the sun and soil nutrients, and those that succeed in doing so will thrive and reproduce. The others die, and other organisms take their place. An environment doesn't tell its organisms how to change so that they will increase their ability to survive. Evolution works by *selection*, not by instruction. The environment *selects* from among the built-in options available to it, it doesn't modify (instruct) the competing organisms.[6]

From Model to Brain. So it is with our brain, Edelman argues. Think of the vast number of highly interconnected neural networks that make up our brain as the neural equivalent of the complex set of jungle organisms that respond variously to environmental challenges. The natural selection processes that shape a jungle over long periods of time also have also shaped our brain over an extensive period, and they shape our brain's neural networks over our lifetime.

Our brain is made up of tens of millions of relatively small basic neural networks, and just as each type of immune antibody responds to a specific environmental antigen, so each sensory network processes a specific element of the external world—a single sound, a diagonal line. Various interconnected combinations of these basic neural networks process more complicated, related phenomena—from sounds to phonemes to words, from lines to triangles to pyramids.

Thus, we have a modular brain, in that a relatively small number of standard, nonthinking components combine their information to create an amazingly complex cognitive environment. For example, when we observe a red ball rolling along a table, our brain processes the color, shape, movement, and location of the ball in four separate brain areas. It's not yet clear how the complex communications among four such areas result in our brain's creation of a unified picture of a rolling red ball—but then, it's also not clear how the members of a jazz quartet communicate with one another as each improvises on a simple theme, blending individual efforts into unified song.

The theory of neural Darwinism argues that genetic processes that evolved over eons of time create a generic human brain that is fully equipped at birth with the basic sensory and motor components a human needs to function successfully in the normal physical world. Our species needs to hardwire its basic survival networks (e.g., circulation, respiration, reflexes), but individuals also need the flexibility of adaptable or "softwired" networks to be able to respond to specific environmental challenges (e.g., to learn French, to drive a car).

An infant brain doesn't have to learn how to recognize specific sounds and line segments; such basic neural networks are operational at birth. We don't teach a child to walk or talk; we simply provide opportunities for adaptations to an already operational process.

Gazzaniga (1992) argues that all we do in life is discover what's already built into our brain. What we see as learning is actually a search through our brain's existing library of operating basic networks for the combinations of those that best allow us to respond to the immediate challenge (much like college students in a library select and synthesize materials from various existing sources to write their term papers).

On the other hand, our DNA couldn't possibly encode our brain's networks for every possible combination of sights, sounds, smells, textures, tastes, and movements that our brain can process, so instead it encodes a basic developmental program that regulates how neurons will differentiate and interconnect. The fetal brain thus develops general areas dedicated to various basic human capabilities within a certain range of variation, such as our ability to process language. Infant brains are born capable of speaking any of the 3,000+ human languages, but they're not born proficient in any of them.

When infants begin to interact with the local language, their brain can already recognize the sounds of the language. The larger neural networks that process the specific language(s) they'll speak form as the various combinations of sounds in the language(s) occur frequently. The amount of use selectively strengthens and weakens specific language networks. The networks for sounds that aren't in the local language may atrophy over time due to lack of use, or they may be used for other language purposes. Scientists call this process neural pruning. We can see its results in the difficulty that most older Japanese adults have with the English *l* and *r* sounds, which aren't in the Japanese language. A Japanese adult who learned English as a child would have no trouble with the two sounds.

To those who argue that they taught their child to speak a language, the theories ask, in effect, "And when and how did you *teach* your child your native accent, prepositional phrases, and the rules for forming the past tense?" Children master most of the complexities of grammar with practically no explicit instruction from their parents, although extensive parent-child verbal interactions obviously provide an important environment for the effective development of a language.

Thus, learning becomes a delicate but powerful dialogue between genetics and the environment: the experience of our species from eons past interacts with the experiences we have during our lifetime. Our brain is powerfully shaped by genetics, development, and experience—but it also then actively shapes the nature of our own experiences and of the culture in which we live. Stimulating experiences create complex reciprocal connections among neural networks. A limited sensory input can thus trigger a wide range of memories, but such memories can also trigger internal fantasies and external explorations.

Parenting and teaching are probably something like *facilitating agents*, but how the new brain theories will eventually reconceptualize such concepts is not yet clear. Hubel (1988) certainly underscored the important role that facilitating agents play in early life experiences when he studied the development of the visual cortex in kittens. Kittens reared in a research environment that lacked certain line orientations (such as vertical or horizontal lines) suffered a dramatic decline in the viability of the neural networks that normally process the type of line orientation that had been eliminated from the kitten's experience—and so they tended to walk into chair legs if vertical lines had been eliminated from their early experience.

Technology as a Solution to Biological Problems. Unfortunately, biological evolution proceeds at a very much slower pace than cultural evolution, so we're forced to grapple with current social and environmental issues using a brain that biological evolution has tuned to the far different cognitive challenges of 30,000 years ago, when physical dangers were signaled by rapid changes in the environment, not by gradually developing problems (e.g., pollution, overpopulation, acid rain).

Part of the difficulty is that evolutionary modifications occur within the existing biological system. Evolutionary processes don't dismantle an existing mechanism, such as our brain, and start again from scratch. Evolutionary modifications may therefore differ considerably from what intelligent engineers might have developed had they redesigned our brain from scratch to meet our current needs (Churchland 1992).

We've compensated by seeking technological solutions to our problems. In effect, we've added a layer of *technological brain* (e.g., autos, books, computers, drugs) outside our skull—a layer that continually interacts with our internal biological brain. But each technological advance also creates new human problems. Our profession will be challenged to reconceptualize formal education as new brain theories evolve, and then to discover how best to reset our brain during its development, so that humans might one day develop sound biological solutions to many technological problems that now seem to defy solution. Chapter 6 explores this issue.

The Biological Nature of Consciousness. Francis Crick focused his attention on consciousness, and neural Darwinism also seeks to define the biological nature of consciousness, an important but formidable challenge for any brain theory.

Edelman divides consciousness. *Primary consciousness* is a state of being mentally aware of objects and events currently in the immediate environment. But these mental images aren't accompanied by any sense of being an organism with a past or future. An animal with primary consciousness sees a room the way a beam of light illuminates it—with an awareness of only the illuminated areas, and with no ability to connect what it sees to other areas. Edelman calls this level of consciousness "the remembered present." Primary consciousness permits the brain to create a complex mental scene that connects the immediate perceptions of a situation to the parts of the brain that process such survival values as food, light, and warmth—and so it takes a subjective (i.e., eat-or-be-eaten) view of everything it confronts.

Higher order consciousness is perhaps a distinctly human condition that allows us to build on primary consciousness, to go beyond it to recognize our own personal actions and values. It uses language and other symbols in processes such as reflection and generalization that can emotionally detach us from the here and now, and lead us into purely imaginative mental scenes. Higher order consciousness suggests a linking of the brain areas that process primary consciousness with the areas of symbolic memory and conceptualization: it adds past and future to the present, and a sense of the inner self to the world out there.

Thus, memory combines a built-in species bias for such values as food, warmth, and survival with current short-term events. Long-term memory is an adaptive (but currently ill-understood) cognitive technique that operates within a single lifetime. It is a necessary capability for directing conscious behavior from within, for moving beyond pure stimulus-response behavior. Further, laws and traditions become cultural memories that can last beyond a single lifetime—perhaps an early first step in genetic change.

Seeking Educational Applications

Finding practical educational applications in Crick's hypothesis and Edelman's theory is difficult. At this point, they are basically science research agendas. Applications to educational policy and practice will come later, after the kind of study that leads to greater understanding.

Edelman's model of our brain as a rich, layered, messy, un-planned jungle ecosystem is especially intriguing, however, because it suggests that a junglelike brain might thrive best in a junglelike classroom that includes many sensory, cultural, and problem layers that are closely related to the real-world environment in which we live—the environment that best stimulates the neural networks that are genetically tuned to it.

The classroom of the future might focus more on drawing out existing abilities than on precisely measuring one's success with imposed skills, encourage the personal construction of categories rather than impose existing categorical systems, and emphasize the individual, personal solutions of an environmental challenge (even if inefficient) over the efficient group manipulation of the symbols that merely represent the solution. Educators might then view classroom misbehavior as an ecological problem to be solved within the curriculum, rather than aberrant behavior to be quashed. The curriculum might increase the importance of such subjects as the arts and humanities, which expand and integrate complex environmental stimuli, and reduce the importance of basic skills and forms of evaluation that merely compress complexity.

Such a *brain-based* curriculum might resemble some current practices, but it might differ considerably from what schools are now doing. It's interesting to muse on such widely acclaimed developments as thematic curricula, cooperative learning, and portfolio assessment. All require more effort from teachers than do traditional forms of curriculum, instruction, and evaluation. Is the appeal to educators that these approaches seem to be inherently right for a developing, *junglelike* brain, even though they require more professional effort and aren't nearly as economical and efficient as traditional forms?

For now, Crick and Edelman and their growing band of fellow brain theorists provide us with rich (and at times junglelike) book environments for professional reading and contemplation. The theories will continue to develop, and educational leaders must enter into the process now, or else biologists may well redefine our profession for us.

HOW OUR BRAIN
ORGANIZES ITSELF
ON THE CELLULAR
AND SYSTEMS LEVELS

From their penthouse location in our body, our brain's tens of billions of neurons and hundreds of billions of glial support cells organize themselves at the cellular and systems levels to efficiently process the information we need to survive and to thrive. Our brain is designed to move information in space and time—from as far out in the starlit sky as our eyes can see to as far away on earth as our legs can walk, from as far back in real time as our memory can recall to as far forward in psychic time as our plans can project.

New brain theory and research seek explanations of conscious and unconscious behavior within the biology of brain cells and systems. This chapter explains some important brain processes that educators should be aware of: (1) what body/brain cellular systems do, (2) how individual brain cells process the molecular units of information that move within and between individual cells, and (3) how our brain organizes itself into large networks of cells that process more complex forms of information and behavior.

The explanations will be stated principally in functional terms that you can use in your work with students, staff, and patrons. Still, this chapter deals with the *geography* of our brain, and it may be difficult reading for you if you have painful memories of trying to learn many place-names during your K–12 school years.

Geography as a concept involves much more than the place-names of the various landforms, bodies of water, and communities that compose our earth. You don't have to know the name of a lake to swim in it, or the name of a mountain to climb it. But you must know the place-names if you want to talk to someone about where you went and what you did. This chapter provides helpful place-name information on the brain cells, organs, systems, areas, and processes that are important to the educative process. These brain terms (and their definitions) will appear in other books and articles about our brain.

If you don't immediately need or want the technical information in a paragraph in this chapter, go on to the next paragraph. The subheads and illustrations, and the index, should help you to return easily to a term and its definition if the discussion in a later chapter requires that information. I've placed the most technical information in the appendixes.[1]

Cellular Systems

Complex collections of cells that carry out mutually supportive structural and transportation functions organize themselves into organs and organisms. Many complex organisms, such as humans, also organize themselves into complex cooperative communities. We unconsciously accept this arrangement as almost definitive of life.

Structural Systems

Most individual cells in our body carry out structural and maintenance functions that complement and supply the adjacent cells in their organ. In effect, we have many cottage industries all over our body that develop such locally needed products as tongue, liver, and fingernails. A fingernail-making cell has to concern itself only with maintaining a steady output of keratin molecules near the tip of a finger. It doesn't ship its product beyond its immediate neighborhood, nor is it conscious of what's occurring on other fingers or elsewhere in the body. It doesn't even know how our brain and body will use the fingernail.

Transportation Systems

Our bone marrow and endocrine glands are examples of the broader cellular systems that use tubular networks to transport their information-laden products throughout our body and brain. They thus create a single, interconnected, functioning organism out of the widely distributed organs encased within the six-pound, 20-square-foot mantle of skin that covers our body. The marrow and glands continually synthesize and discharge numerous red blood cells and hormones into the 60,000 miles of blood vessels that constitute our circulatory system.

Our circulatory system transports each blood cell or hormone molecule to any of numerous sites in our body prepared to receive it. It's a simple system that creates a whole body/brain response to a whole body/brain problem, such as "I'm hungry" or "I'm scared." Because it takes only a minute for each heartbeat of blood to move throughout our body, all the necessary organs quickly receive the nutrients and hormones they need to carry out their small part of the larger task at hand. This general distribution system operates much as you would if you were walking down the street with the intent of giving a $10 bill to the first 12 red-headed people you meet. You know you'll eventually hand out the bills, but you can't predict who will get them.

If you want a specific red-headed friend to get a $10 bill, however, it's better to send it by direct mail than to walk the streets in the hope of meeting your friend. Neurons operate under this kind of system, a specific distribution system. Neurons contain tubular extensions designed to communicate very quickly with specific cells within complex networks. When a phone rings, it often takes less than a second for individual neurons in our auditory network to integrate the ringing sound with specific neurons in other networks that process related memory and problem-solving strategies, and then to activate the specific muscle fibers that carry out the task of picking up the telephone.

Our brain uses these two sets of transportation systems to unconsciously regulate most of our body's systems—within established schedules, cycles, and limits that cover most of our needs. Examples abound: heartbeats, the onset of puberty, menstrual cycles, levels of pain and pleasure, the ten-octave range of the human auditory system.

An information system that functions automatically can persist in its programmed flow of information when our conscious brain doesn't want it to, such as when a throbbing headache interferes with reading a book. Our brain has developed internal chemical override systems that use complex *peptide molecules* to modulate the negative effects of such persistent conditions. For example, enkephalin and dynorphin are peptides that our brain produces to reduce the effects of extraordinary pain.

Our conscious brain may choose not to wait for such unconscious processes to function at the level it desires, or it may decide they are inadequate to deal with the current real or imagined problem. Our conscious brain can then override, supplement, speed, or slow the production and distribution of its own natural chemical information systems by seeking out and taking in herbal or synthetic molecules that have the power to create the internal mental state that our conscious brain desires. These molecules are the psychoactive drugs, and they can affect how our body/brain processes and transports information (Chapter 6 discusses the effects of psychoactive drugs).

Brain Cells and Chemical Messengers

Our brain is composed principally of neurons (nerve cells) and glial support cells. Neurons appear to be the principal cellular agents of cognition, but the less-understood glial cells play active roles in at least several key areas of brain development and maintenance (Kimmelberg and Norenberg 1989). Various molecules carry messages throughout our brain and body, generally from one neuron to another.

Glial Cells

Glia means glue, and glial cells were originally thought to be the glue that holds our brain together. In fetal brain development, star-shaped glial cells do act as a scaffold of sorts that newly formed neurons use in migrating from the brain areas where they were created by cell division to the specific sites where they will carry out their appropriate neural functions. Thus, glial cells play a very important role in establishing the general architecture of our brain.

Our brain must tightly control the chemical balance within its cells, because chemical imbalances can result in mental illness. Glial cells assist in this task by forming part of the blood-brain barrier that surrounds capillaries, thus denying entry into our brain to many unnecessary or dangerous molecules that travel in the bloodstream. Glial cells also help to regulate our brain's immune system and to metabolize the two key neurotransmitters in the cerebral cortex, GABA and glutamate (discussed later in this chapter). A neurotransmitter is a molecule released by neurons to transmit messages to other cells.

Glial cells also form an insulating layer (myelin) around the nerve fibers that send messages to distant cells, and this insulation increases the speed and precision of such neural messages. Multiple sclerosis is a disease resulting from the deterioration of the myelin sheath. Glial cells are also involved in many developing brain tumors.

Neurons

Our brain processes messages within an information network that includes our brain, sense organs, muscles, and glands, but most messages involve neuron-to-neuron communication. Only a few million of our brain's tens of billions of neurons have sensorimotor connections with our body. A neuron constantly receives messages from and sends messages to other cells. The chemical decision to send a message depends on whether the current amount and type of input have reached the neuron's threshold for output.

Neurons are beautifully designed to carry out their functions. We have only to look to the human arm for an image of the neuron's three main parts: the hand represents the neuron's cell body; the fingers, its dendrites; and the arm, its axon. Figure 2.1 shows the main parts of the neuron.

Cell Body. A neuron's cell body contains all the structures that maintain cellular functions. An individual neuron can remain functional throughout our lifetime, but it rebuilds itself every three months or so, molecule by molecule, as parts wear out. The cell body and its DNA genetic system use the nutrients that the blood brings into the cell to maintain the cell and to synthesize the neurotransmitter molecules that are central to its communication with other cells.

A neuron may interact with thousands of other cells, some of them quite far away (in cellular terms). Therefore, the cell body contains separate sets of tubular sending and receiving extensions (axons and dendrites) that keep the neurotransmitter molecules and their information within the neuron's body as they are transported to specific neurons in the labyrinth of our densely packed and chemically complex brain. The neuronal extensions in a cubic centimeter of brain tissue would extend an astounding 400 miles if they were spread out in one line!

Dendrites. A typical neural cell body contains many short, fingerlike, tubular extensions called dendrites that receive information from other neurons. Dendrites can extend a millimeter or so into the surrounding area, which doesn't seem like much until you recall that 30,000 neurons can fit into a space the size of a pinhead. Dendrites contain many *receptors*—protein molecules that extend through the dendrite's membrane to receive the chemical message carried by another neuron's neurotransmitter molecules. Spines may develop on dendrites during memory formation, increasing the number of receptors and therefore the amount of neurotransmitter information that can enter the neuron at one time. Figure 2.2 shows different sorts of neurons and their dendrite development.

Axon. A typical neuron has an axon extension that sends the neuron's message to the other neurons in its circuit. As noted in Chapter 1, motor neuron axons can extend a meter, but most axons are in the millimeter range. Because the myelin insulating layer on

FIGURE 2.1
FUNCTIONAL MODEL OF A NEURON

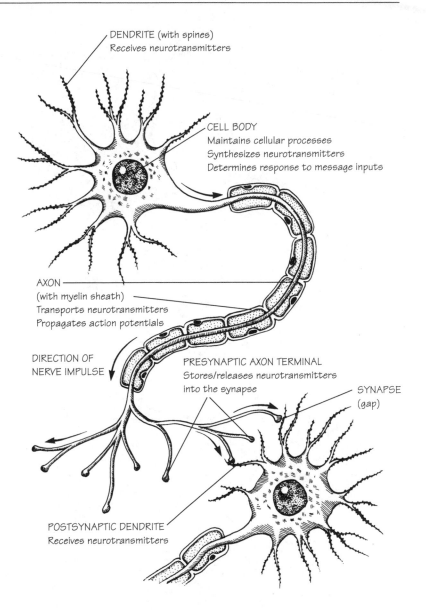

DENDRITE (with spines)
Receives neurotransmitters

CELL BODY
Maintains cellular processes
Synthesizes neurotransmitters
Determines response to message inputs

AXON
(with myelin sheath)
Transports neurotransmitters
Propagates action potentials

DIRECTION OF
NERVE IMPULSE

PRESYNAPTIC AXON TERMINAL
Stores/releases neurotransmitters
into the synapse

SYNAPSE
(gap)

POSTSYNAPTIC DENDRITE
Receives neurotransmitters

FIGURE 2.2
VARIATIONS IN NEURONS

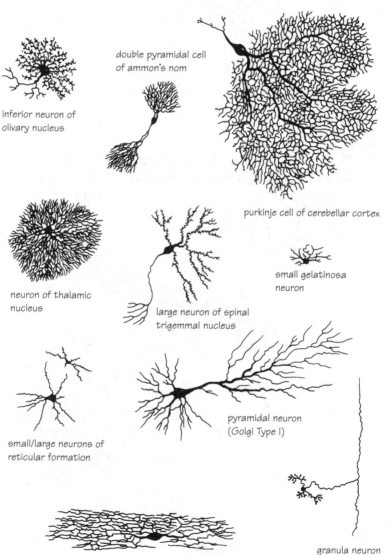

double pyramidal cell
of ammon's nom

inferior neuron of
olivary nucleus

purkinje cell of cerebellar cortex

small gelatinosa
neuron

neuron of thalamic
nucleus

large neuron of spinal
trigemmal nucleus

small/large neurons of
reticular formation

pyramidal neuron
(Golgi Type I)

spindle-shaped neuron of substantia gelatinosa

granula neuron
of cerebellum

long axons is white, the term *white matter* is often used to describe the large areas of brain tissue composed principally of myelinated axons. An axon may divide into branches toward its end, and thus send its message to many other neurons. The ending of an axon branch is called a *terminal,* and it is here that a neuron stores its neurotransmitters in little packets called *vesicles* while they wait to be released.

Chemical Messengers

The information that neurons process is coded into chemical molecules called *neurotransmitters* and into the distribution patterns of these molecules. Molecules are formed from two or more atoms. In our brain, the principal atoms are carbon, oxygen, nitrogen, and hydrogen. Between 10 and 30 atoms join to form one of the 20 different amino acids that are the building blocks of our brain's protein, hormone, and neurotransmitter molecules.

The Language of Amino Acids. The amino acids that make up a protein molecule are assembled in a linear sequence within a cell (following genetic directions coded into the DNA in the cell's nucleus), and this chain then twists itself into a characteristic globular shape before leaving the cell to carry out its intended protein functions. The whole process takes only a few minutes. The pattern of electronic properties that arises out of a molecule's shape determines the effect it will have on cells and other molecules.

Twenty amino acids can create hundreds of thousands of different protein molecules in the same manner that 26 letters can create an English language of 500,000 words. The information in proteins or words is coded not into the amino acids or letters themselves, but into their sequence and the length of the chain. For example, neither D nor O carries useful verbal information by itself, but DO creates a verb. Add G and the verb DO becomes the noun DOG. Reverse the letters and DOG becomes GOD. Insert another O and the noun GOD becomes the adjective GOOD. Add an S and the noun GOODS emerges.

We usually do not read the individual letters of a word, but instead perceive the shape of the entire word as a unit—and then transduce its visual shape (sequence of letters, length) into a sound sequence that we can pronounce as a word. A wrong letter in a word results in a different word (CAT/COT) or a spelling error

FIGURE 2.3
SYNAPTIC AREA

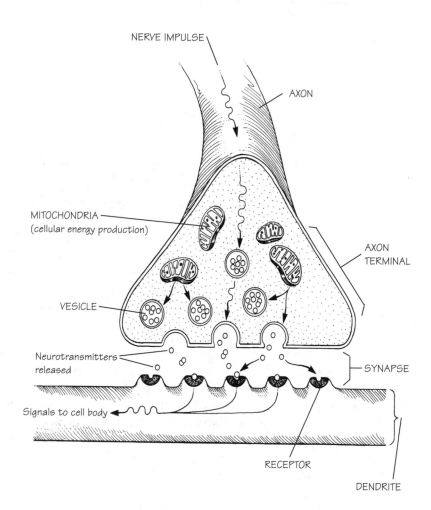

(KAT). Similarly, placing an amino acid in a different position on a protein chain can change the protein, cause a genetic illness, or both. For example, sickle-cell anemia is a *genetic spelling error* that occurs when the amino acid valine is substituted for glutamic acid in one position on the 300-amino-acid sequence that constitutes the hemoglobin half-molecule (hemoglobin is the coloring matter of red blood cells).

It's difficult to understand how our brain can combine a curved line, two diagonal lines, two horizontal lines, and one vertical line into a shape that creates a mental representation of CAT; it's equally difficult to understand how the electronic properties that emerge out of the shape of a molecular clump of amino acids can communicate specific organic information.

The Actions of Neurotransmitters. Scientists have already identified more than 50 neurotransmitters and will probably identify more before the entire system is understood. Neurotransmitters carry out their various communicative functions at the *synapse,* a very narrow gap that separates the axon terminal of a presynaptic neuron from the dendrites of a postsynaptic neuron (see Figure 2.3). The postsynaptic dendrites contain receptors—protein molecules that project through the dendrite's membrane. Think of a receptor as a lock, and a neurotransmitter as a key. The shape of the neurotransmitter (key) interacts with the shape of the receptor (lock). If it's a good match, the neurotransmitter transmits its message into the postsynaptic neuron.[2]

If, as explained briefly below and in Appendix A, the number and intensity of the various messages simultaneously entering a postsynaptic neuron reach the neuron's firing threshold (think of a thermostat), the chemical message translates into an impulse that rapidly opens and shuts channels as it travels along the axon. Each channel opens the next channel in line, like each domino pushing over the next domino in a line of falling dominoes. When the neural impulse reaches the presynaptic axon terminal, it releases neurotransmitters into the synapse, where they cross to the postsynaptic dendrites, and the communicative process continues from neuron to neuron.

Our brain's dozens of types of neurotransmitters can be classified both functionally and chemically. Appendix A provides additional information on the neurotransmitters described briefly here.

A Functional Classification of Neurotransmitters. A neurotransmitter sends either an excitatory or inhibitory message to the receiving neuron. An excitatory message helps to increase the subsequent communicative actions of the postsynaptic neuron, and an inhibitory message helps to reduce them. Think of an on/off switch or the binary number system. The chemical composition of the neurotransmitter interacting with its target receptor determines the nature and complexity of the message.

Why do our brain's neurons need dozens of different types of neurotransmitters to communicate two basic messages: *Do it* or *Don't do it*? Perhaps for the same reason that our language has dozens of verbs to express the basic message *Move your body by moving your legs,* when the verb *walk* expresses the basic idea. Words like run, dance, hop, jog, and skip add information to the basic concept. Think also of the modulating effects of adverbs on verbs, and adjectives on nouns. Similarly, the variety and complexity of excitatory and inhibitory neurotransmitters probably add some form of currently ill-understood supplementary information to the basic molecular message.

Neural activity in our brain is fortunately much more inhibitory than excitatory. At any moment, we focus our attention, limit our activity, and ignore most of our memories. Imagine life with a principally excitatory brain that continually attended to everything, carried out all possible actions, and had continual open access to all prior experiences!

A Chemical Classification of Neurotransmitters. Our brain's 50^+ neurotransmitters can be chemically classified into three types:

Amino Acids. Four chemically simple amino acids form one class of neurotransmitters. Glutamate (or glutamic acid), an excitatory neurotransmitter, and GABA, an inhibitory neurotransmitter, are the principal neurotransmitters used by the neurons in the cerebral cortex, which occupies 85 percent of the mass of our brain.

Monoamines. Dopamine, serotonin, and norepinephrine are examples of a half dozen chemically modified amino acids that form a second class of neurotransmitters. Think of each monoamine system in terms of a small lawn sprinkler that distributes water to a large lawn area. Each type of monoamine neurotransmitter is synthesized in the neurons of one brainstem or limbic system source and is then spread throughout our brain, where it helps to combine the activities of related brain areas. In the cortex, the monoamines modulate the actions of glutamate and GABA (rather than act as primary agents of transmission).

Peptides. The largest and most complex neurotransmitters are the peptides (or neuropeptides), such as endorphin and vasopressin, composed of chains of 2 to 39 amino acids. Most of the dozens of types of neurotransmitters in our brain are peptides, but the concentration of each is lower than that of the amino acids and monoamines, which are known as the *classical neurotransmitters.* Many neurons that synthesize a classical neurotransmitter also synthesize a peptide that modulates the actions of the classical neurotransmitter.

Peptides use neural networks, our circulatory system, and air passages to travel throughout our body/brain to modulate our broad range of pleasure and pain. Thus, they powerfully affect the decisions we make within the continuum of emotionally charged *approaching* and *retreating* behaviors, such as to drink-urinate, agree-disagree, buy-sell, and marry-divorce. In effect, the shifts in the body/brain levels of these molecules allocate our emotional energy: what to do, when to do it, and how much energy to expend.

At the cellular level, peptides synthesized in one cell attach to receptors on the outside of another, sparking increases or decreases in various cellular actions that can affect our overall emotional state if the action occurs simultaneously in large populations of cells. Cell division and protein synthesis are two such actions, and both are heavily involved in the emotion-charged body changes that occur during adolescence (Moyers 1993).

A peptide's message can vary in different body/brain areas, just as a two-by-four can be used in many different ways in the construction of a house. Angiotensin is a peptide that activates the seeking and conserving behaviors that regulate our body's fluid levels. In our brain, it does this principally by activating feelings of thirst and the consequent behaviors that seek water. In our body, it causes our kidneys and lungs to conserve water. The situation is similar with many drugs. For example, alcohol can excite or sedate, depending on the amount ingested and the drinker's emotional state.

Because the peptides play an important role in modulating emotional states and consequent behaviors, they are especially significant to educational policy and practice. Cortisol and the endorphins are two good examples of peptides that can affect behavior in educational settings.

Cortisol illustrates the complexity and adaptability of the peptide system, in that it is the all-purpose wonder drug that our adrenal glands distribute when our inability to fend off danger leads to a stress response. Cortisol activates important body/brain defensive responses that vary with the nature and severity of the stressor, but all such responses protect our body from physical danger (e.g., bleeding, tissue damage) because our stress response developed eons ago, when survival was most threatened by physical dangers. Thus, our stress mechanisms don't differentiate between physical and emotional danger. Since most contemporary stress results from emotional problems, our stress responses are often maladaptive.

For example, suppose a 2nd grader refuses to complete an arithmetic assignment, and the irritated teacher's stress system inappropriately responds through defenses tuned to physical danger—by releasing clotting elements into the blood, elevating cholesterol levels, depressing the immune system, tensing large muscles, increasing the blood pressure—and much more. This response makes sense only if the recalcitrant student also has a knife or club.

We pay a high cost for chronic emotional stress. Low cortisol levels lead to the euphoria we feel when we're in control, but high cortisol levels provoked by stress can lead to the despair we feel when we've failed. Further, chronic high cortisol levels can lead to the destruction of neurons in the hippocampus associated with learning and memory (Vincent 1990), and even the short-term stress-related elevation of cortisol in the hippocampus can lead to an inability to distinguish between the important and unimportant elements of a memorable event (Gazzaniga 1988a). Thus, school environments that cause continual stress reduce the school's ability to carry out its principal mission. Chronic stress can also lead to a variety of circulatory, digestive, and immune disorders.

On a more positive molecular note, the endorphins are a class of opiate peptides that act to modulate emotions within our pain-pleasure continuum, reducing intense pain and increasing euphoria. Exercise and positive social contacts, such as hugging, music, and the supportive comments of friends, can elevate endorphin levels and thus make us feel good about ourselves and our social environment (Levinthal 1988). Joyful classroom environments that encourage such behaviors create an internal chemical response that can increase the possibility that students will learn how to solve problems successfully in potentially stressful situations.

Brain Systems

Various models of our brain's architecture have been proposed over the years, but they've tended to become more reductionist. Thus, the earlier idea of a holistic brain gave way to an intense cultural interest in the two cerebral hemispheres, which gave way to Paul MacLean's (1978) model of a triune brain, a three-layer, hierarchical brain that evolved to process survival, emotional, and rational functions. More recently, Howard Gardner (1983) has suggested that our conscious brain functions through seven forms of intelligence processed in different brain areas. Gazzaniga (1985) continued this reductionist pattern by suggesting that our brain is divided into a vast number of interconnected, semi-autonomous networks of neurons that he calls modules. Each module specializes in a limited cognitive function (such as one aspect of face recognition), and groups of modules consolidate their activities to process more complex cognitive functions.

Because MacLean's triune brain model is easy to understand, it has been widely used, especially in education circles. Recent discoveries suggest, however, that it's probably more useful as a functional metaphor of our brain's organization than as an exact model (Cytowic 1993). Cognitive scientists currently seem to favor a modular brain organization that has less of the hierarchical flavor of MacLean's model, and that increases the importance of the limbic system (the emotional center of our brain).[3] This discussion will therefore focus on the modular organization of our brain. The illustration in Figure 2.4, however, draws on MacLean's familiar triune brain model to help orient you to the location of various structures.

A Modular Brain: Basic Organizational Patterns

Multiplex Processing. Information in our brain flows in multiplex patterns that involve not only parallel neural circuits, but also peptides and hormones that flow in the fluids surrounding the neurons and their extensions. Parallel processing means that many

FIGURE 2.4
MacLean's Triune Brain Model

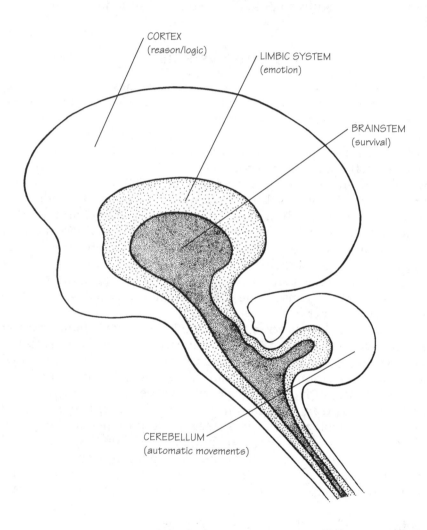

CORTEX
(reason/logic)

LIMBIC SYSTEM
(emotion)

BRAINSTEM
(survival)

CEREBELLUM
(automatic movements)

Adapted from Paul MacLean, "A Mind of Three Minds: Educating the Triune Brain," in Education and the Brain, edited by J. Chall and A. Mirsky (Chicago: University of Chicago Press).

conscious and unconscious actions occur simultaneously, within circuitry that includes all sorts of interconnections and feedback loops. Communication in our brain moves more in the parallel pattern that spreads a rumor throughout a community (via personal contacts, phone, mass media, etc.) than in the linear sequence that moves a letter through the postal service. At some level, everything seems connected to everything else.

An example of this type of complex conscious/unconscious processing occurred to me just now, and I'm sure you've also experienced it: A name I had tried to recall an hour ago suddenly popped into my mind. Although I had put the name out of my conscious thoughts, some unconscious brain circuits evidently continued to search for the name after I had shifted my attention to this manuscript, and then demanded to report it to my conscious brain when they located the name—whether or not I still wanted the information.

Distributed Processing. Our brain's neural networks are distributed, in that many brain areas (or modules) combine to process an event or object. For instance, the act of looking at a person's face involves the several brain areas responsible for processing the various spatial, color, and movement elements constituting a face. Further, each such brain area processes its specific task within many different and larger tasks. For example, the network that processes a specific property, such as the color red, processes that color in all objects containing it.

Marcus Raichle (1993) suggests the modular brain analogy of a symphony orchestra with its various sections and instruments. In an orchestra, no unique combination of players and instruments constitutes a C Major chord. Rather, many potential combinations can produce the chord. Each combination creates a somewhat different sound, but every one of them is a legitimate C Major chord.

At the neural level, think of distributed processing in terms of the light bulbs that switch off and on in an advertising sign that constantly changes its message. A given bulb will light up as a part of many different letters, digits, and words. Similarly, a neuron can be a part of many different actions and memories.

The concept of a modular brain suggests a librarian/library model of our brain's organization and operation that you might find useful. Our brain carries out many of the same informational

FIGURE 2.5
SCHEMATIC MODEL OF BRAINSTEM AND LIMBIC SYSTEM

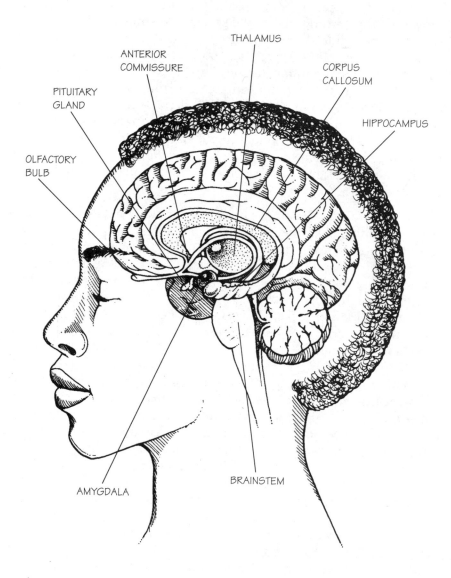

functions for our body that a librarian and library materials carry out for a school. The discussion to follow will develop this functional model.

All models, including this one, contain elements that distort reality, so models shouldn't be viewed as anything but a simplified functional approximation of reality. For example, this library model will compare neural networks to books, but we must bear in mind that the pages in a book passively receive their printed information, while the neurons in a network actively participate in the processing of information.

Internal and External Systems

Our brain must focus both on our internal needs and values and on our interactions with the external world, and so it divides these tasks between two interrelated systems (Edelman 1992).

A System for Internal Needs and Values. The finger-sized brainstem at the base of our brain and the limbic system structures surrounding it create a value-driven system that focuses inward on our survival, emotional, and nurturing needs. (For a rough visualization of the combined limbic/brainstem system, cut a slice about the width of a finger out of a bagel and then slip your index finger into the cut-out space and balance the bagel on your extended finger. For a more detailed picture, see Figure 2.5.)

Extensively connected in looped circuits to body organs and systems, our limbic/brainstem system responds relatively slowly (in periods from seconds to months) as it regulates basic body functions, cycles, and defenses, including circulation, respiration, appetite, digestion, sexuality, and fight-or-flight behaviors. Many of its structures appear to be programmed very early for the roles they will play in our life, and we can't easily change them once they're set. Our temperament and emotions simply exist. We don't *learn* them the same way we learn a telephone number. We can learn how to use rational processes to override our emotions if a situation requires that we do so, but our actual *feelings* about the situation usually do not change.

Several educationally significant structures play especially important roles in our limbic/brainstem system:

The Reticular Formation. Located at the top of the brainstem, the reticular formation integrates the amount and type of incoming

43

sensory information into a general level of attention (Vincent 1990). Our level of attention fluctuates in 90-minute cycles each day, but our average attention levels are generally highest in the morning after we wake up; they drop during the day and evening, and dip below consciousness at night when we're asleep (Hobson 1989). The term *reticular* means *net*, and that's a good way to think of the system, as a chemical net that opens and closes to increase and decrease the information flow in and out of our brain. All sensorimotor information flows through our brainstem.

In our library model, budgets, patron demographics, and checkout procedures all help to determine and regulate what enters and leaves a library.

The Limbic System. Folded around the brainstem is the limbic system, which is composed of several interconnected olive- to walnut-sized structures that emerge out of the cerebral cortex. Loaded with peptide receptors, it's our brain's principal regulator of emotions. It also influences the selection and classification of experiences that our brain stores as long-term memories. It's powerful enough to override both rational thought and innate brainstem response patterns. We tend to follow our feelings.

Because the limbic system plays important roles in processing both emotion and memory, emotion is an important ingredient in many memories. Memories formed during a specific emotional state tend to be easily recalled during events that provoke similar emotional states (Thayer 1989). Thus, family arguments and happy occasions tend to spark the recall of similar arguments and happy times. Similarly, classroom simulations and role-playing activities enhance learning because they tie curricular memories to the kinds of real-life emotional contexts in which they will later be used.

Research suggests that the *amygdala* is the principal limbic system structure in emotional processing (Aggleton 1992). The amygdala complex is composed of two almond-shaped, fingernail-sized structures that are richly and reciprocally connected to most brain areas, especially advanced sensory-processing areas. Its principal task is to filter and interpret sophisticated incoming sensory information in the context of our survival and emotional needs, and then to help initiate appropriate responses. Thus, it influences both early sensory processing and higher levels of cognition (e.g., ignoring the feel of a comfortable shoe, but responding to a shoe with a tiny pebble in it).

The amygdala adjoins the *hippocampus,* two integrated finger-sized structures that appear to convert important short-term experiences into long-term memories. Think of the amygdala and hippocampus as processing the same kinds of selection and classification tasks with our memories that a librarian performs with books and other materials. A librarian (with input from staff and students) subjectively selects the materials to add to the library collection, and the amygdala (with input from many other brain areas) subjectively selects the experiences we decide to remember.

In effect, the hippocampus and its connections objectively classify and store the selected memories in appropriate memory networks elsewhere in our brain. Thus, we can functionally think of the hippocampus as the card catalog for our library of memories. Alzheimer's disease involves a breakdown of hippocampal neurons, and so its onset signals the gradual loss of *access* to one's memories. In our library model, it would involve the gradual loss of cards from the card catalog, rather than the loss of books. The loss of a few cards isn't serious, but the loss of many cards creates a dysfunctional retrieval system.

The Thalamus and Hypothalamus. The walnut-sized *thalamus* and adjoining olive-sized *hypothalamus* are related limbic system structures that assist in regulating our emotional life and physical safety. The thalamus is a major relay center for incoming sensory information, and so it informs our brain about what's happening outside our body. The hypothalamus monitors our internal regulatory systems, and so it informs our brain about what's happening in a variety of systems and organs inside our body. For example, if our blood contains too much salt, the hypothalamus initiates a search for water to dilute the concentration; if our blood contains too much sugar, the hypothalamus suppresses our appetite. Sexual orientation is another internal value regulated by the hypothalamus, and the small neural structure in the hypothalamus that does this is larger in males than females. A recent study found that male homosexuals tend to have the neural structure typical of the opposite gender. Thus, our sexual orientation may not be as freely chosen as some people believe (LeVay 1993, LeVay and Hamer 1994).

When our rational/emotional brain structures can discover no appropriate solution to a threatening situation, our hypothalamus can activate a fight-or-flight stress response through its pituitary gland contacts with the endocrine gland system.

45

FIGURE 2.6
SCHEMATIC SIDE VIEW OF CORTEX

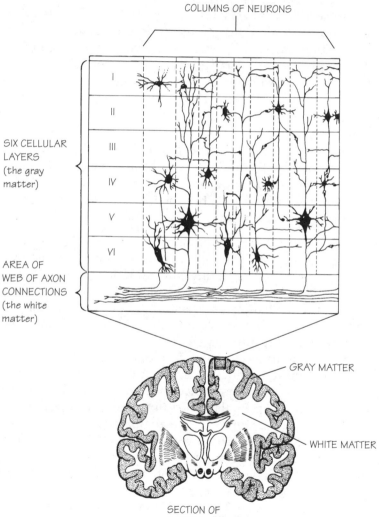

COLUMNS OF NEURONS

SIX CELLULAR
LAYERS
(the gray
matter)

I

II

III

IV

V

VI

AREA OF
WEB OF AXON
CONNECTIONS
(the white
matter)

GRAY MATTER

WHITE MATTER

SECTION OF
CEREBRAL CORTEX

A System for External Challenges. The cerebral cortex (or just cortex) is a large, divided, six-layer sheet of neural tissue that folds deeply around the limbic system. It occupies 85 percent of our brain's mass and, when spread out, approximates the area and thickness of a stack of six sheets of 12" x 18" construction paper (or a large dinner napkin). You can create a simple brain model (showing cortex, limbic system, and brainstem) by placing these six sheets of construction paper on top of a bagel with the small bit cut out of it and then slipping your index finger into the cut-out space and balancing the bagel on your extended finger).

The cerebral cortex is organized into a myriad of highly inter-connected and outwardly focused neural networks that respond very rapidly (in milliseconds to seconds) to various spatial and temporal demands. The system (1) receives, categorizes, and inter-prets sensory information, (2) makes rational decisions, and (3) ac-tivates behavioral responses. In our library model, the cerebral cortex is equivalent to the library building itself because the cortex stores and retrieves the memories that represent the objects and events of the external world.

Cortex means *bark* (as in tree bark), so one could think of our cerebral cortex as the bark of our brain. A side view of the cortex (shown in Figure 2.6) reveals six distinct cellular layers created by the size, shape, and density of the neural cell bodies that predomi-nate in each layer in the cortex. This cellular part of the cortex is called the *gray matter.*

The cortex is organized into several hundred million neural net-works (or modules), most of which are arranged in vertical col-umns of neurons (each about the thickness of a thin sewing needle) that extend through the six cortical layers. Each such column (of about 100 neurons) processes a very small segment of a brain func-tion, such as responding to a specific unit of sensory information in the surrounding environment (a line segment, a tone, an odor). Adjacent columns may combine to form a module that processes more complex aspects of the function. Axons extend down the col-umn through the cellular layers, then move horizontally along the *white matter,* a dense web of axon connections beneath the gray matter. Eventually, the axons leave the white matter to connect with neurons in a related nearby column or to project into another brain area.

Figure 2.7
Schematic Top View of Cortex

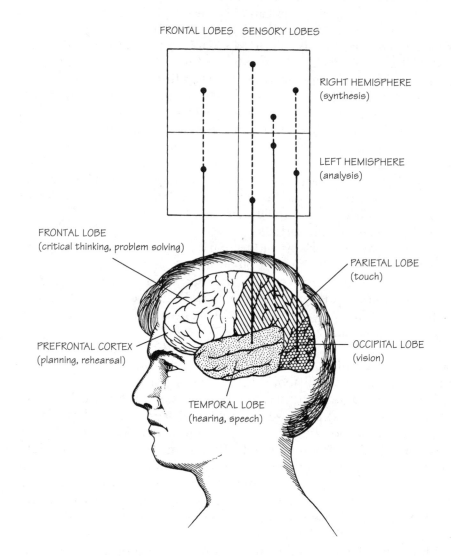

FRONTAL LOBES   SENSORY LOBES

RIGHT HEMISPHERE
(synthesis)

LEFT HEMISPHERE
(analysis)

FRONTAL LOBE
(critical thinking, problem solving)

PARIETAL LOBE
(touch)

PREFRONTAL CORTEX
(planning, rehearsal)

OCCIPITAL LOBE
(vision)

TEMPORAL LOBE
(hearing, speech)

Such complex patterns of connected columns allow sounds to become phonemes to become words to become sentences to become stories—and all the other complex cognitive behaviors that are created from combinations of basic columnar units. Many scientists believe that these columns, not individual neurons, are the fundamental unit of the structure of our cortex (Wills 1993).

Think of the columnar networks as books in a library. Each book focuses on one topic (just as each cortical column processes a single type of information). Nearby books on a shelf are similar, not identical, but the set of similar books contains the library's basic information on that topic—just as the cortical columns that focus on related types of information are located near one another. A book's bibliography connects it to related books in the library—and axon extensions connect a column to related columns nearby and in other brain areas.

A top view of the cortex provides a general sense of where various things are processed, and the dramatic advances in brain-imaging technology will certainly move scientists beyond their current knowledge of the geography of our cerebral cortex. Think of the top view of our cortex as something like the layout of a library: fiction is placed here, history is there, and science is over against that wall. The principal processing tasks of the cortex involve objects and events in space and time. As shown in the simplified top view of the brain in Figure 2.7, objects and events in space are processed along the right-to-left axis of the cortex, and objects and events in time are processed along the back-to-front axis.

Right-to-Left Organization: Space. Viewed from the unfolded top, the cerebral cortex is divided into right and left hemispheres along a line running directly back from our nose. The 200+ million axons of the *corpus callosum* and *anterior commissure* connect neural columns in the two hemispheres. Although differentiation of tasks (lateralization) does occur, the hemispheres collaborate on most tasks, and the corpus callosum helps to synchronize their activities. For example, the left hemisphere (in most people) processes the objective content of language—*what* was said—while the right hemisphere processes the emotional content of facial expressions, gestures, and language intonation—*how* it was said. By processing related information from different perspectives, the hemispheres collaborate to produce something that becomes a unified mental experience.

Think of the functional roles our hemispheres play in terms of our brain's need to synthesize and analyze, to simultaneously see the entire forest and one of its individual trees. If you close your eyes for a few moments and then quickly open them, you'll instantly see everything in your visual field, but most of what you see will be the basic lines and edges that make up the shapes. You'll get a general background (or cartoon) view of the scene, rather than a detailed view.

Now focus your attention on one object and intensely examine it. Imagine what kind of a brain you would need to instantly process that much detailed information from all the objects in your several sensory fields. It would be a very large, high-powered, and inefficient brain confronted with a continuous overload of information. Everything would become foreground, and so you wouldn't be able to focus your attention on anything.

Thus, our brain must have one set of mechanisms that instantly see the forest—that *synthesize* the background or context by gathering a little bit of high-contrast information from each of many units in our sensory fields. Synthesis provides a quick, general sense of what's out there and how all those units are related. For most people, the right hemisphere specializes in this task. It's been called our metaphoric mind because metaphors, parables, maps, graphs, cartoons, and so on provide only the outlines of a broad concept that can be experienced and interpreted in many ways.

Conversely, the left hemisphere of most people contains the mechanisms that *analyze* the individual foreground elements of our broad sensory fields—by carefully examining the lower contrast details of an individual tree, while the right hemisphere monitors the entire forest. This analysis must be done sequentially, because our brain can't simultaneously examine several individual trees in different areas of our visual field. Thus, our left hemisphere is designed to process information that must be processed sequentially.

As noted earlier, human language is a sequential process. Because we code most of our information into differing sequences of letters and words, not into the letters themselves, our left hemisphere is generally the principal processor of spoken, written, and signed language.[4] Because a word packs considerable information into a few relatively similar sounds or symbols, our comprehension of it requires close attention to subtle shifts in sound and line orientations that are characteristic of left hemisphere processing.

It's important to realize that we humans made a major leap in the power and flexibility of communication when we assigned the content of our communication to letter sequences of varying lengths (words). In so doing, we created language. Primates use about three dozen distinct sounds in their communication, each signaling a specific meaning, such as anger, fear, or food. We took about the same number of sounds, removed the meaning from them, and turned the sounds into multipurpose phonemes that could be combined and re-ordered in sequences of varying length to form our complex language of 500,000 specific, meaningful words.

Stringing things together appears to be a key function of our brain. We string notes into songs, and steps into dances. We string events into stories, and actions into games. Joining things together in sequences adds flow to our life. And it's as basic to life itself as the stringing together of amino acids into the chains that make the proteins that create and maintain our body.

The research on the roles the hemispheres play in emotion is inconclusive, but some general patterns have emerged (Corballis 1991). The right hemisphere appears to play the more prominent role overall, especially in men, possibly because emotion is more a synthesis than an analysis of information. The right hemisphere processes the negative aspects of emotion that lead to withdrawal behaviors (e.g., fear, disgust), while the left hemisphere processes the positive aspects that lead to approaching behaviors (e.g., laughter, joy). Strong feelings tend to be negative, probably because it's more important for the brain to communicate that a problem exists than to say that everything is okay.

As suggested above, the average male brain appears to follow this pattern of hemisphere specialization, while the average female brain may diffuse more emotional processing across the two hemispheres (Moir and Jessel 1991). If so, this organizational difference may help to explain commonly observed gender differences in emotional processing. Men, who tend to restrict language processing to their left hemisphere and most emotional processing to their verbally silent right hemisphere, may have more difficulty than women do in talking about their feelings and instead may express them through gestures, gifts, or sports. Further, men tend to experience more difficulty than women in recovering language capabilities after a left hemisphere stroke.

Gazzaniga (1992) suggests that our brain contains an important interpreter function that is also located principally in our left hemisphere (probably because of its close relationship to analytic and language functions). Our brain's interpreter creates reasonable explanations (and rationalizations) for events that are otherwise difficult to explain. These emerge out of our personal experiences, and so may differ from the inferences and explanations of others. Thus, this interpreter function is central to our belief system and self-concept. It leads to religious resolve, political activism, fears, arguments, diets, and a whole lot more.

Back-to-Front Organization: Time. Foreground and background have a somewhat spatial conceptual orientation, but our brain must also confront the temporal dimensions of problems. Events occur in the present, but they often result from previous events and they lead to future events. Our brain's principal concern is to identify and respond to potentially beneficial or harmful environmental changes, and much of this problem-solving activity is centered in our cerebral cortex. We must be able to draw on our past experiences and predict what might occur in the future if we are to avoid becoming a prisoner of the absolute present, viewing each current problem as a novel challenge.

Our cortex is thus organized to integrate the past, present, and future into the solution of current problems, dedicating major areas to the various processes that constitute memory (past), critical thinking and problem solving (present), and planning and rehearsal (future). Our brain's ability to rapidly integrate these temporal functions suggests that the highly interconnected mechanisms are spread across the cortex, but both the location and maturation of specific functions suggest the following general organization also exists: the back of the brain handles the past; the middle, the present; and the front, the future. The Piagetian stages of cognitive development roughly divide the maturation of the cortex, with the earlier-developing sensorimotor and concrete operations stages concentrated in the back half, and the later-developing formal operations stage concentrated in the front half.

The Past: Memory. Our cortex is divided into two hemispheres, and each hemisphere is divided into four lobes. The lobes occupying the area roughly behind a line drawn from ear to ear process sensory information and memories: the *temporal lobes* (above and behind our ears) process hearing and speech; the *occipital lobes* (at the back of our head) process vision; and the *parietal lobes* (at the top of our head) process touch and motor control. Important connections combine sensory information and memories, so that when we hear the word *banana*, we can see and feel a banana in our mind, even though no banana is present. These sensory lobes represent the past in this discussion because they process the existing categories that humans must master. A child asks what something is, and the parent responds with the appropriate nouns and adjectives that have evolved over time. Thus, children are introduced to the past—and they store many of these sensory facts in the back half of their cerebral cortex. (Chapter 3 focuses on our sensory system.)

The Present: Critical Thinking and Problem Solving. Our brain has more *frontal lobe* capacity than we normally need to survive because the critical-thinking and problem-solving mechanisms located there must be sufficient for crisis conditions (just as furnaces must be able to function well on the coldest day of the year).

Since our survival doesn't require our problem-solving mechanisms to operate at capacity most of the time, we've invented social and cultural problems to keep them continually stimulated and alert. The arts, games, and social organizations provide pleasant metaphoric settings that help to develop and maintain our brain's problem-solving mechanisms. They are not trivial activities—in life or in the curriculum. Jean Piaget's suggestion that play is the serious business of childhood attests to the important developmental and maintenance roles that such activities have in mastering problem solving. During times when many personal or vocational problems beset us, our frontal lobes are all booked up with business, so we tend to limit our social and entertainment activities.

Our brain's critical-thinking and problem-solving mechanisms are especially effective at rapidly processing ambiguities, metaphors, abstractions, patterns, and changes as they create and confront concepts. They can categorize 100 leaves as maple leaves, even though no two of the leaves are identical, and they can recognize a classmate at a 25th reunion, despite all the physical changes that have occurred. Our brain's critical-thinking abilities permit us to succeed in a world in which most of the problems we confront require a quick, general response rather than detailed accuracy. Thus, we can quickly classify objects we confront into general categories and estimate general solutions to our problems. We then adapt our preliminary decisions to any new information we might gather, using reference materials and machines to achieve further levels of precision.

We call it intuition, common sense—and we depend on it for much of what we call problem solving. It can lead to mistakes and to the overgeneralizations of stereotyping and prejudicial behavior, but also to music, art, drama, invention, and a host of other human experiences that open us to the broad exploration of our complex world.

The frontal lobes play an important role in regulating our emotional states and judgments. Our frontal lobes' regulation of critical thinking and problem solving permits us to override the execution of automatic behaviors and potentially destructive, illegal, or immoral behaviors sparked by emotional biases.

The Future: Planning and Rehearsal. Mechanisms in the prefrontal cortex, located right behind our high forehead in the front part of the frontal lobe, permit us to plan and rehearse future actions, to take risks in our brain's mental world rather than in the real world. The prefrontal cortex is responsible for budgets, hotel reservations, and lesson plans. It's the final part of the cortex to mature, during our late adolescence.

Our brain's ability to predict events is crucial to scientific thought, but it also leads to the worrying we do about the future. If we can worry about our future, however, we can also worry about the future of others and the future of our environment. Consequently, our prefrontal cortex (with its strong limbic system connections) also regulates important elements of our emotional life—feelings of empathy, compassion, altruism, and parenting.

*   *   *

Our brain is organized to respond to a wide variety of challenges from its inner and outer environments. We seem most comfortable when we're in the cognitive center, where things are neither too simple nor too complex and emotion reigns supreme, where trees meld easily into the forest and we're satisfied with the focus of our attention, where the present is comfortably continuous with the past and future.

We don't have a perfect brain, but it's certainly excellent—fearfully and wonderfully made, as an early contemplator of the human condition poetically put it.

HOW OUR BRAIN
INTERACTS WITH THE
OUTSIDE ENVIRONMENT

Our brain is not a part of the external environment. Imprisoned and protected within the darkness and silence of our skull, it depends on its sensory and motor systems for external access. Our sensory and motor systems developed to enhance survival, but our conscious brain also uses them to reach out and explore cultural interests and abstract diversions—to smell flowers, observe sunsets, thrill to thunder, run races, throw Frisbees.

In *The Republic* (Part Seven, Book Seven), Plato related the Allegory of the Cave, which provides us with an intriguing, almost mythical introduction to our sensory and motor systems. (And in the process, Plato also conceptualized both compulsory education and the film theater a couple of thousand years before we got around to working out the details.) Plato described a group of people who had been chained within a cave in a manner that prevented them from looking out, that forced them to look inward at the cave's back wall. A large fire burned outside the mouth of the cave, and when anything passed between fire and cave, it created flickering shadows on the back wall—shadows that provided the cave dwellers with information from the otherwise unseen outside world.

The cave's information system reduced the outside world's complex, colorful, three-dimensional visual reality to simple, two-dimensional, black-and-white shadow representations of whatever happened to pass between fire and cave. It wasn't much, but the cave dwellers watched the wall with great interest, since it was their only access to the outside world. Over time, they became quite adept at interpreting these shadows, and at ascribing deeper meanings to the limited representations they could observe. But their chains left them helpless to directly experience the outside world.

The Allegory continues its exploration of the nature of reality and representations of reality through the experiences of a cave dweller who escaped his sensory shackles and moved out of the cave into the sunlight of pure ideas, into the difficult search for a true understanding of the actual nature of the outside world. It thus provides a vehicle for exploring the problem our brain has of knowing how to interact effectively with an outside world that is a layer of bone and skin away from the three pounds of brain tissue that's trying to understand it. Think of our skull as Plato's cave, our sense organs as the fire at the entrance that sends shadowy representations of the outside world into our brain's sensory lobes (located, interestingly, toward the back of our brain). Think of our brain's neural networks as the cave people—at the mercy of sense organs that can send only limited representations of reality into the skull that holds the brain that's trying to figure out what's going on *out there.*

And yes, extend your thoughts also to classroom *caves*—with students metaphorically chained to their desks, looking at the chalkboard up front that's filled with vertical, horizontal, diagonal, and curved lines that the curriculum combines into very limited verbal representations of just about everything that exists beyond the classroom walls.

All external sensory impressions register on the millions of specialized receptors in either the 6-pound, 20-square-foot mantle of skin that covers our body or the sense organs embedded in our skin. Our brain and skin are thus closely related. They are the first two organs to emerge in the developing embryo. About two weeks after conception, they begin to develop out of the same layer of embryonic tissue: the cells on one side develop into skin, and those on the other side become brain. We might therefore consider our skin the outside layer of our brain because it's where our brain meets the outside world.

Our sensory receptors monitor the surrounding environment for specific changes in the composition and movement of molecules and light rays that strike our body—changes in temperature, air and physical pressure, reflected light rays, and the chemical composition of air, water, and food. Further, they focus on changes within relatively narrow ranges: about 130 degrees on the Fahrenheit scale, 30 or so odor-related molecules, 10 sound octaves, 4 food properties, and the narrow band of visible light in the broad electromagnetic spectrum. These changes in the surrounding environment may not seem like much, but they are the primary source of all the information our brain gets about what's happening outside our skull. An exceptional sense of taste and smell can provide a wine taster with a vocation, and psychedelic drugs can briefly expand parts of our sensory range, but our sensory system is genetically quite limited.[1]

Limitations make sense. Our brain couldn't possibly process all the information the surrounding molecules and vibrations carry. We've always been curious about what exists beyond our sensory range, however, so we've developed such technological extensions as microscopes, telescopes, and oscilloscopes that transduce inaudible sounds into visible patterns.

Computers have materially broadened our knowledge of the universe by expanding the range and precision of such sensory technology. The curriculum should help students understand and master this technology, but it should also examine the social value of the information that lies beyond our brain's limitations. For example, a computerized camera can now identify the winner of a race by differences of hundredths of a second, when our visual system and less precise brain would have called it a dead heat. The curriculum should encourage students to ask questions like these: How important is such accuracy to the human spirit when a race is but a game? Does precise information become important simply because it's technologically available?

Chapter 2 reported that the thalamus is our brain's initial processor of external sensory information, and the hypothalamus is the monitor of most of our body's internal changes. Our body's various endocrine balance systems and immune defense mechanisms are also linked to our brain, and so we can view them as part of a general internal sensory/regulatory system that helps to keep us upright, and that recognizes and destroys harmful substances that enter our body.

We are, therefore, a body bombarded by a rich blend of initially meaningless molecular fragments and light rays that represent complex outside and inside environments—*flickering shadows* that enter our brain and modify the neural networks that consciously and unconsciously analyze and synthesize our relationships with our environment.

Our sensory system operates through two distinct pathways: a fast system that provides information on *where* the object is located and a slower system that indicates *what* the object is.[2] We can perhaps best see this system at work in our response to pain, which occurs when a stimulus is more intense than the sensory system can tolerate. The first message to reach our brain is about the pain's location (right foot) and the second message is what caused the pain (a tack).

Thought often leads to a decision to act, and our jointed motor system with its complex brain-muscle connections provides our brain with a remarkably effective external mechanism for action. It's composed of the toe, foot, and leg system that is about half our body's length; the finger, hand, and arm system that extends about two feet beyond our body; a flexible neck that increases the geographic range of our head's sensory receptors; and a mouth that begins digestion and communicates through both sound and movement (facial expressions). Still, we can run only so fast and jump only so high. Some people devote years of their youth to trying to jump an inch higher than anyone else has ever jumped. Other people use a ladder.

It's really quite remarkable what our brain can do with such limited sensory and motor systems. Let's first examine them functionally, and then biologically.

Our Sensory System

The Functions of Our Sense Organs

We can sequence our sense organs by their reach for information, from those that gather and process information inside our body to those that reach out well beyond our body.

As indicated earlier, the air and fluids coursing through our body's complex systems of tubes carry a wide variety of life-sustaining and life-threatening substances. Our body's immune system identifies and destroys bacterial and viral antigens, and our brain's hypothalamus maintains internal stability (homeostasis) by monitoring and regulating the concentrations of a variety of life-sustaining molecules in our body fluids.

Our tongue is appropriately located right below our nose and eyes. We can view it as a protective trapdoor that provides a final taste check on food before it enters our 30-foot-long digestive system. Its receptors monitor two chemical properties that are necessary to life (salt, sweet) and two that signal danger (sour, bitter). Other sensory receptors in our tongue, teeth, and mouth provide important information on the temperature, texture, and hardness of the food we plan to eat.

The large waterproof mantle of skin covering our body looks inward to help keep our insides in place, heat in, and infection out. But it also looks outward to report on the weather and on the shape and size of the things we touch.

If our tongue and skin were our only sense organs, we would walk right past food we didn't touch or walk right into danger, so it's important to have other senses that let us know what's in the vicinity before we actually touch it.

Our sense of smell alerts us to nearby objects and organisms through molecules they release into the air that attach to receptors in our nose. Because odors travel through the air, we can tell that the source of the odor is in the vicinity, but we may have trouble locating it. Further, smell provides no information on size and shape. Vision and hearing solve such problems in that they permit our brain to locate objects at a distance—in the daylight and unobstructed, and in the dark or obstructed. The doubling of eyes and ears adds sensory depth, enhancing our brain's ability to create an external impression of the object at its location, a significant sensory advantage. Vision and hearing are the only two senses that allow our brain to psychologically leave its skull. We see and hear the object or event at its location, not inside our brain where all cognition really takes place.

Our sense organs bring important information into our brain, but they also communicate many things about ourselves and our values to other people. The visible parts of our skin, hair, nails, and teeth are all dead tissue, but we expend inordinate time and energy in trying to make them look alive. Perhaps it's the mortician in us. We support entire industries dedicated to this cosmetic compulsion to attract the attention of others. We rearrange skin and teeth, trim hair and nails, wash with special soaps and creams, dab on sweet-smelling perfumes and deodorants. To no avail. What others see of us is still dead. Life is within.

Nevertheless, we use our skin and other sense organs both to communicate and to hide what's happening in our brain and body. We add cosmetics to increase or decrease our apparent age or to compensate for perceived shortcomings in our appearance. We use such built-in facial cosmetics as frowns, grins, and yawns to display our inner feelings. Our eyes *sparkle, look tired, spit fire.* We shout in anger and laugh in joy. We gently communicate our love through caresses and kisses.

Others can infer much about our race, gender, state of health, approximate age, occupation, habits, and values concerning cleanliness by carefully observing our head and hands (the two parts of our body we tend to leave uncovered). They can infer even more from our clothing, the principal extension of our skin. Like skin, most clothing is made of dead material (cotton, wool, leather, and chemical synthetics). Because clothing, jewelry, and glasses provide a far more flexible communicative tool than skin, we can use this second layer of skin to communicate even more of the values and vitality hidden in our brain and body. For example, military people in full uniform symbolically drape their entire professional biographies on their body.

Social categorization can arise out of such surface communication—the hurt that comes from racism and sexism, the help that comes from recognizing a police officer when we need one. Adolescents have long realized that the best way to keep adults at a distance is to wear bizarre clothing and hair styles and to bombard adults with loud, atonal music. Mass media and mass culture thus combine to set surface styles for people who want to identify a group—or to identify with a group.

Think now about a third layer of skin—our housing and classroom walls. Like skin and clothing, such walls keep our possessions in place, help maintain an appropriate temperature, and protect us from danger. But they also communicate much about ourselves and our values. The furnishings that gradually fill our homes are histories of our lives. Some classroom walls are filled with marvelous curricular windows that explore the world beyond the walls—and with curricular mirrors that reflect values and activities back on the teachers and students. Some walls communicate excitement. Some invite touching. Some breathe life. Others just stand there, a stack of dead building materials.[3]

The Biological Structure of Our Sense Organs and Receptors

Let's move now from the functions of our sensory system to its biological structure, looking at our sense organs and their brain connections in a sequence that roughly reflects their level of emphasis in school activities (the reverse of the inside-to-outside functional sequence).

Our sensory system includes (1) the receptors that transduce sensory input into neural codes and (2) the rest of the sense organ and brain processes that collaborate to transform this seemingly unconnected and meaningless information into complex forms of integrated knowledge. The simple descriptions here will give you a basic idea of how our sense organs function.

Our Eyes. The site of 70 percent of our body's sensory receptors, our eyes begin the cognitive process of transforming reflected light into a mental image of the objects that reflected the light. Light rays (photons) enter an eye through the system of the cornea, iris, and lens, which focuses the image on the thin retina sheet at the rear of the eyeball. The rays are absorbed by the retina's 120 million rods and 7 million cones, with each rod or cone focusing on a small, specific segment of the visual field. Rods process the dimly lit, peripheral, black-and-white, moving elements of the image; the centrally located cones process the clearly lit, detailed, colored elements. (The rich color spectrum we can see results from the combined actions of only three kinds of cones that respond to red, blue, and green wavelengths.)

The light rays absorbed by a rod or cone cause a chemical reaction that stimulates related retinal neurons to begin the process of combining the input of individual receptors into a complex image. In effect, the retina takes a rapid and continuous series of still pictures of the eye's visual field (much like a motion picture, which is made up of still pictures shown in a rapid sequence that creates the perception of motion).

Our visual system is designed to focus our brain's attention principally on movement and contrast (lines, edges, contours, spots), and generally to merely monitor static solid areas. Thus, written languages are composed of combinations of vertical, horizontal, diagonal, and curved lines that seem to draw the eyes along rather than cause them to rest on one area.

The one million fibers in the optic nerve of each eye carry a summary of the vast amount of data that the 127 million rods and cones receive. Half the optic fibers from each eye cross over to the opposite side of our brain, joining the remaining fibers from the other eye and continuing to the thalamus, our brain's initial sensory-processing area and relay center (located in the middle of our brain). Thus, each side of our brain receives visual information from both eyes.

The information is next relayed (1) to the amygdala in the limbic system, for emotional analysis, and (2) to the visual cortex, two credit-card-sized areas in the occipital lobes at the back of our brain, where columns of neurons are arranged to respond to specific patterns of lines, angles, segments, and movements in the visual field. Further processing (forward in the cortex) combines line segments into shapes, colors them, combines them, locates them in space, names them, and contemplates their meanings. At this point, sensory processes are being transformed into thought processes.

Think of your eyes as the projector lens, and your visual cortex as the screen that registers the rapid sequence of sunlight-to-starlight still pictures it has received from your retina—still pictures that it translates into a continuous mental motion picture that functions magnificently beyond mere flickering shadows on the wall at the back of a cave.[4]

Our Ears. Unlike our eyes, our ears have no "lids" to shut out stimuli. The ears are our brain's 24-hour monitoring service. They can pick up potentially important information from behind a wall, in the dark, or across relatively large distances.

Hearing is a three-phase action that creates useful cognitive information out of the pitch, volume, and timbre of complex sound waves that vibrate through air, bone, and fluid. The process begins in our outer ear, where sound waves strike our ear drum and cause it to vibrate. Our middle ear increases the strength of these vibrations about 22 times through the mechanical actions of the three smallest bones in our body (commonly called the hammer, anvil, and stirrup). They relay the increased vibrations to the cochlea, a fluid-filled tube in the inner ear shaped like a snail shell. Each of the 25,000 hairlike receptors in the cochlea is tuned to a specific sound frequency. If the sound wave moving through the fluid bends a receptor, it activates a neural message at a specific frequency that the auditory nerve then sends to the temporal lobe of our brain.

The auditory nerve contains a nerve fiber for each of the cochlear receptors, whereas the optic nerve contains a nerve fiber for every 127 rods or cones. These different ratios may explain why our brain mixes yellow and blue to get green, but hears all the notes in a chord. Like the optic nerve, the auditory nerve runs through our brain's sensory relay center in the thalamus and divides so that both ears connect with the auditory processing centers located above both our ears.

Our brain can recognize about a half million different sounds across ten octaves, but it can't process all possible sounds (e.g., very soft sounds). We distinguish between pleasant and unpleasant sounds, music and noise—but such judgments are often quite personal. We have many different kinds of music and musical instruments, and our 3,000 languages vary somewhat in the sounds they use, but all human music and languages use the same basic set of sounds—an example of human unity within nature's complexity.

Our Skin. Our skin has more than half a million nerve endings that provide our brain with immediate information on just about anything that touches our body, even a mosquito landing. Our hand has 1,300 nerve endings per square inch. Across our body, a patch of skin the size of a quarter averages more than 3,000,000 cells, 250 sensory receptors, 100 sweat glands, 50 nerve endings, and 3 feet of blood vessels. Our body's 6-pound, 20-square-foot, two-layer mantle of skin is the largest and least-compact of our sense organs. While the other sense organs are only inches away from our brain, information from the skin on our feet, for instance, travels several feet to reach our brain.[5]

The epidermis is the constantly renewing outside layer of our skin. It replaces itself about once a month, as living cells gradually move to the surface, where they form a hard, waterproof cover about 15 cells thick. Protective oils keep the cells pliable, but the top layers constantly flake off.

The dermis is our skin's thicker inside layer. It contains nerve endings, hair roots, sweat or oil glands, and blood vessels. Fibroelastic tissue allows our skin to maintain its tight, smooth cover, and a layer of fatty tissue beneath the dermis attaches the skin to our body. This layer of fat also provides an emergency food supply, acts as insulation to conserve body heat, and cushions our body from bumps and blows.

Various specialized receptors register variations in skin temperature and pressure. Our skin has about 10 times more cold receptors than hot receptors. Some receptors respond to intense pressure and others to gentle stroking. Receptors located adjacent to hair roots monitor hair movements. Pain is initially useful because it alerts us to a threat, which can result from intense changes in temperature and pressure and from skin cuts. We subjectively perceive pain as sharp, dull, throbbing, or shooting, and do what we can to turn it off, once we've responded to the problem. As indicated earlier, our brain produces endorphin peptides to reduce intense pain, and many of the drugs we've developed reduce or eliminate pain.

Touch information and motor output are initially processed in the cortex in two adjacent narrow bands of neural tissue that spread from ear to ear across the top of our cortex. The right side of these sensorimotor bands processes touch and motor activity from the left side of our body, and vice versa. The bands also represent our body areas upside down: sensorimotor activity in our toes is processed at the top of our head, and activity in our tongue is processed down near our ears. Further, the area devoted to a body part is proportional to its sensorimotor complexity and importance, not its size: our hands and face and especially our thumb and tongue get the most space. Macho types may be shocked to discover that their thumb and tongue are their most important appendages, but that's the way things are in the world of brain priorities.

The lengthy human birth process that squeezes the body through a relatively narrow birth canal helps to activate our skin as a functioning organ. The postbirth licking that many animal mothers give to their more easily delivered young serves the same function. Our sense of touch develops early and is stimulated by a child's gentle and positive physical contact with the surrounding environment—by cuddling and hugging, molding clay, running in the breeze, playing catch, finger painting, taking things apart and putting them together. Children must physically interact with objects in their environment in order to understand them, and the school can make a major contribution to this development through hands-on activities. Tactile stimulation is like rubbing the world on the outside layer of our brain.[6]

Our Nose. Our nose processes our sense of smell through two postage-stamp-sized mucus membranes at the top of the nasal air passages. Each membrane has millions of hairlike neural endings that project into the mucus. These receptors interact with odor-bearing molecules that have entered our nose and are trapped in the mucus. Our sense of smell is unique, therefore, in that its receptors are bare neural endings; when we smell something, our brain is in direct chemical contact with the outside world. The system is also unique in that the neurons projecting into the mucus membrane are the only neurons that can regenerate themselves (and they do so every few weeks).

Only a very small amount of the air we breathe passes over these receptors, but our sense of smell is powerful enough to respond to very light concentrations of odor-bearing molecules. Most animals have a much more powerful and directional sense of smell than we have.

Perhaps 30 different molecules are involved in the thousands of different odors we can recognize. Most odors are combinations of molecules that simultaneously enter our nose in the air we breathe and then attach to receptors. It's difficult to classify smells, but seven primary odors have been identified: minty (peppermint), floral (roses), ethereal (unscented nail polish), musky (musk), resinous (camphor), acrid (vinegar), and putrid (rotten eggs).

Smell is the only sense that doesn't pass through the sensory relay center in the thalamus. The initial odor-processing centers, the olfactory bulbs, have major connections with the limbic system, our brain's emotional center. Smell plays an important role in the formation and recall of emotion-laden memories, but we can't mentally recall the odor of an absent object, such as the odor of a rose or an orange, in the same way that we can recall their shape and color. Smell is more important than taste in our recognition and selection of many foods.[7]

Pheromones are powerful hormonelike molecules that animals and humans release from their skin into the air. They enter the tiny vomeronasal organ in our nose, but they are not part of our sense of smell. Rather, we might consider them a sixth sense. They trigger neural activity in areas of the hypothalamus that regulate sexual behavior and levels of comfort and self-confidence. A female moth emitting pheromones can draw male moths to her from miles away. In humans, pheromones have been tentatively associated with such curiosities as the allure of certain perfumes, the attraction of truffles (and their relationship to underarm sweat), and the tendency of women who live together to develop synchronized menstrual cycles. The cheek area next to our nose contains many pheromones, and this may explain why we humans like to kiss by nuzzling our nose into that pheromone-rich area. Although scientists currently know little about human pheromones, one can muse on their possible effects on hundreds of adolescent students, bound together for hours in the enclosed environment of the school.

Our Tongue. Perhaps more important to educators for its role in articulation than its role in eating, our tongue is a four-inch-long mobile slab of muscle with 9,000 taste buds arranged in groups of about 100 on raised projections (papillae) located mostly on the perimeter of its upper surface. Taste buds report only on food that is soluble in water, so saliva is necessary for our sense of taste.

The front of our tongue processes the sweet and salty tastes of foods that help our body maintain proper levels of glucose and sodium, which are important in our brain's metabolic and information-processing functions. The back part of the tongue processes sour and bitter tastes. Our tongue and mouth also register temperature, touch, and pain. Although our brain receives these messages separately from taste, it combines the total sensory message into a complex, integrated flavor sensation: smooth hot chocolate or crunchy peanut brittle. The early maturation of this important sensory integration is evident in the behavior of infants, who examine almost everything they pick up by putting it in their mouth. Fetal taste buds respond to amniotic fluid chemicals by the third trimester.

Our sense of taste is as social as it is biological in that we generally prefer to eat and drink with others. Eating and drinking are major elements in many celebratory and romantic events—even though the basic biological process involves little more than pouring a daily ration of about two gallons of food and water into our 30-foot digestive tube.[8] Eating is much more than taste. It's a rich mix of all the senses: the cooking aromas, the tactile crunch of celery and apples, the attractiveness of the food on the table, the sounds of popcorn, and the flow of conversation. Most people eagerly select from a wide range of tastes and textures, even though a cynic may suggest that most of it comes down to nothing more than variations on pizza—some kind of a bread base with toppings—whether it's called sandwich, pancake, crepe, pie, layer cake, or lasagna or whether it's sliced and shaped into Chinese noodles or Italian pasta. We thus celebrate similarity in diversity when we eat—with each other, with all our senses.

Educators should use the kind of imaginative thinking that transforms mundane multiplication tables into interesting activities to transform hurried, assembly-line cafeteria meals into experiences that celebrate rather than denigrate our sensory system.

Our Motor System

Life moves within our body through a complex system of digestive, circulatory, respiratory, and neural tubes. Our motor system, too, is composed of appendages shaped like tubes, and we travel in moving tubes that we call cars and airplanes. To live is to move, and although moving about in tubes suggests constraints and purposeful efficiency, much human movement has an antic and unrestricted air about it. Many of our dances, games, exercises, and vacation trips celebrate the pure joy we feel in moving about with no serious purpose in mind.

Although billions of neurons may be involved in a decision to move, only about a half million motor neurons are actually involved in activating the muscle groups that make up almost half our body weight—that is, the more than 650 skeletal muscles that connect pairs of bones, and the heart, intestine, tongue, and eye muscles that do other wondrous things. Thus, the visible aspects of our brain's motor system are dependent on a complex cognitive support system. Let's functionally examine our motor system by comparing it to an airline.

The pilot of a commercial airliner is generally seen as the most important person in a flight sequence. The pilot, however, gets paid principally for flying the first and last few minutes of a flight. The automatic pilot does much of the flying between takeoff and landing, while the pilots monitor the instruments. Further, the flight itself depends on a large and less visible support staff who do the preliminary work of purchasing and maintaining airplanes, planning routes and schedules, and handling reservations and ticket sales.

Our motor system has an analogous three-part arrangement. Many sections of our brain, especially the frontal lobes, are involved in the thinking and planning processes that lead to a conscious decision to move, such as to walk to a nearby store. Our conscious starting, walking, and stopping actions are processed principally in a much smaller area of our brain called the basal ganglia. Our cerebellum at the lower back of our brain (our brain's equivalent to an automatic pilot) takes over the routine repeated walking actions shortly after we consciously begin, and so most of our walk to the store becomes an automatic act. Our basal ganglia (along with other brain areas) monitor the trip, and resume conscious control when conscious movements are required (say, to cross a busy street or to walk around an obstruction), much as the live pilot takes over from the automatic pilot when flight conditions warrant it.

This shifting back and forth between conscious and automatic movements is very useful in that it frees our conscious brain from routine actions so that we can converse with a friend, think, and enjoy the view during the walk—things we couldn't easily do if we had to consciously direct our feet with right-foot, left-foot, right-foot, left-foot commands during the walk. Or imagine if we had to consciously move our tongue, lips, and face while we talked![9]

People with Parkinson's disease suffer from neuronal death in the basal ganglia area. Their brain can decide to walk, but they can't consciously initiate the appropriate movements. They can generally continue to walk if someone gets them started, but they can't consciously fine-tune their movements or stop when they want to. The brain areas that regulate planning activities and automatic movements function, but it's as if the pilots didn't show up to take off and land the planes in an otherwise functioning airline.

Recent technological developments that materially increase the range and speed of human movement and communication pose analogous educational issues about the conscious and automatic movements of students.

Our brain's motor system drives the communication skills that dominate the curriculum. Relatively complex brain mechanisms and muscle groups control the mouth and hand movements that we use in interpersonal communication. Our voices are directed to hearing, and hand and finger movements primarily to vision (generally via paper). Both muscle groups are most efficient when they function automatically—when our conscious brain can focus on the content of the message rather than on the vehicle of expression.

Thus, we have long taught cursive writing because its automatic, flowing nature permits writing speeds between 15 and 30 words a minute. But with much less instruction time, elementary students can learn to touch-type well beyond that speed, and the superb editing and spell-checking capabilities of word processors will be readily available for any extended writing students will do throughout their lives. These developments suggest that we should phase out cursive writing as our principal technique for extended automatic writing. Rather, we should teach elementary students to compose stories and reports directly on word processors, and to use manuscript or cursive writing primarily for short notes and forms. Composing on a keyboard, like writing with a pencil, is an acquired skill. Its speed and rhythm are often more attuned to the speed of thought processes than is cursive writing. Indeed, writing composed directly on a word processor tends to become more flowing and conversational in style.

Developments in oral communication technologies further complicate this issue. In our increasingly oral society, one could ask whether it's important to be able to quickly type a document that will be sent via fax or e-mail when communication via the telephone and its answering machine are even faster. Voice input and output capability in computers is developing rapidly, and while its advent will be a boon for handicapped students, it will also create curricular adjustments for those with normal language proficiency. For example, clear diction and correct syntax will likely be more important when we speak to computers than when we speak to people, whose brains can more easily adapt to errors in speech and syntax.

These developments are still in the future. What's really terrible right now is that more than 25 years after the appearance of the word processor, schools are still mostly dependent on pencils—on pencils without spell-checkers that rapidly report errors and so actually improve the writer's spelling, on pencils (with their little pink rubber delete buttons) that punish writers for writing tentative thoughts by forcing them to rewrite an entire page rather than simply replace a word or a section. We continue to teach elementary students manuscript and cursive writing, but not touch-typing—at an age when they can easily master it. We may complain that our communities won't fund the hardware, but practically all businesses are now computer-driven. Only our schools are still pencil-driven.

*   *   *

We began this chapter with an outside-to-inside sensory system that constantly receives a multitude of individual, meaningless inputs from the surrounding environment, and we end with an inside-to-outside motor system that consciously and unconsciously activates specific muscle fibers that may be more than six feet from our brain. In between these sensory beginnings and motor endings are complex cognitive processes that create subjective meanings from objective sensory inputs and subjective motor responses to an objective environment. The chapters that follow describe these complex in-between cognitive processes.

4

HOW OUR
BRAIN DETERMINES
WHAT'S IMPORTANT

E motion and attention are the principal preliminary processes that our body/brain uses in its efforts to survive (and
even to thrive) in the face of continual challenges. Our
wary brain constantly surveys our internal and external environments to determine what's important and unimportant. Emotion provides a quick, general assessment of the situation that
draws on powerful internal needs and values (to survive, eat, nurture, and mate), and attention provides the neural mechanisms that
can focus on the things that seem important, while monitoring or
ignoring the unimportant.

Our emotional and attentional mechanisms are ancient, quick,
and powerful. They evolved to rapidly size up and respond to
imminent predatory danger and fleeting feeding and mating possibilities—better to flee unnecessarily many times than to delay once
for a more detailed analysis of the threat, and so die well informed.

Chapter 2 described the neural systems that regulate emotion
and attention. This chapter focuses more on the functional elements of those systems and on their educational applications.

Emotion

Our profession pays lip service to educating the whole student, but school activities tend to focus on the development of measurable, rational qualities. We measure students' spelling accuracy, not their emotional well-being. And when the budget gets tight, we cut the difficult-to-measure curricular areas, such as the arts, that tilt toward emotion.

We know emotion is very important to the educative process because it drives attention, which drives learning and memory. We've never really understood emotion, however, and so don't know how to regulate it in school—beyond defining too much or too little of it as misbehavior and relegating most of it to the arts, PE, recess, and the extracurricular program. Thus, we've never incorporated emotion comfortably into the curriculum and classroom. Control and accountability aren't as central to emotion as they are to school.

Recent research developments are unlocking the mysteries of how and where our body/brain determines what it likes, merely tolerates, and avoids. The emotional system emerging from this research is a complex, widely distributed, and error-prone system that defines our basic personality very early in life and is quite resistant to change.[1]

Body/Brain Processes

LeDoux (1994) calls emotion the conscious product of an unconscious process, but our emotional responses aren't the primary business of the body/brain systems that generate them. Our emotions result from triggering systems of behavioral adaptation that have evolved over eons of time. They've allowed our species to survive, so they've become very powerful.

Damasio (1994) differentiates between primary and secondary emotions. Primary emotions include innate responses to stimuli that have a high potential for danger—loud noises, sudden looming shadows. We're probably not genetically programmed to fear snakes, but rather to attend to oscillating (snakelike) movements. We acquire secondary emotions through experience—the feelings we have upon getting or losing a job, hearing a favorite song, and driving in heavy traffic.

Chapter 2 described our emotional system as being regulated by (1) a widespread system of powerful peptide molecules that carry ill-understood emotional information, and (2) body and brain structures and systems that activate and regulate our emotions. The principal brain structures appear to be the limbic system (especially the amygdala) for primary emotions, and specialized cortical networks in the right hemisphere and frontal lobes for secondary emotions and for modulating the more primal emotional responses of the limbic system.

Far more neural fibers project from our brain's relatively small limbic emotional center into the large logical/rational cortical centers than the reverse, so emotion is often a more powerful determinant of our behavior than our brain's logical/rational processes. For example, purchasing a lottery ticket is typically an emotional decision, not a logical one. (The odds are terrible, but where else can one buy three days of fantasy for $1?) We can override our emotions with logical/rational processes, but doing so rarely changes our real feelings about the issue at hand.

Our emotions allow us to assemble life-saving information very quickly, and thus to bypass the extended conscious and rational deliberation of a potential threat. Most incoming sensory information is sent first to the thalamus, and then it's relayed to the sensory and frontal lobes (in the cortex) for detailed analysis and response. A second, quicker pathway also sends any emotionally laden information from the thalamus to the amygdala (in the limbic system), which uses primitive general categorizations of the limited sensory information it has received to activate an immediate aggressive or defensive response, if the stimulus is sufficiently strong. This activation of the sympathetic nervous system to a fight-or-flight stress response engages our entire body—the endocrine, immune, circulatory, muscular, and digestive systems.

As indicated above, this quick, emotionally loaded (but perhaps also life-saving) response is often triggered before we consciously know very much about what's actually occurring. Thus, stereotyped information can lead to irrational fears and to prejudicial and foolish behaviors that we may later regret when we get more detailed and objective information from the slower cortical analysis. Our wary brain believes that it's probably better to over-respond to potential danger than to ignore it (and, in the category of "Responding to Fleeting Food Possibilities," to purchase a lottery ticket every week because "This *might be* the week I win").

Emotion, like color, exists along a continuum. If we travel the color spectrum as it gradually moves from red to violet, we note the subtle shifts in color, but we can also stop here and there and identify discrete primary and secondary colors. Such factors as context, hue, and brightness can also affect our perception of a color: we can perceive an object as blue against one background, and as green against another. So it goes with emotions. We can easily identify many discrete emotions through their standard facial and vocal expressions, but the intensity level and meaning of the emotion will vary among people and situations. In the classroom, most points on the continuum are apt to be represented at any given time—a rich emotional symphony. We're fascinated by emotion because it plays like music—constantly changing its tone, intensity, rhythm. And like most song lyrics, the basic message focuses on a point somewhere along the pleasure-pain continuum.

An emotional response can occur at almost any point along the continuum, but the response tends to be strongest toward either end. A sudden unexpected danger, such as a loud sound or a serious accident, can quickly escalate us along the continuum to an explosive emotional response. But the situation can also develop gradually, such as a series of minor misbehaviors that finally moves us to the threshold of explosive exasperation over something quite minor. Many classroom and family eruptions occur this way. The tragedy is that these slowly developing eruptions can generally be avoided, because the participants have enough time to insert reason into the equation while negative emotions are only simmering.

Emotion also has an important positive side that can move life beyond mere survival into a much more pleasant sense of joie de vivre. Infants are born with the ability to cry and smile, which they quickly develop, and they soon discover that smiling has a better internal and social payoff. Many of our emotionally stereotyped facial expressions (such as crying and laughing) trigger the release of endorphins and other peptides that enhance the emotion in us and in those around us. We may accept grief, but we tend to move toward those things that give us joy—music, games, jokes, dances, caresses, sunsets, celebrations, vacations.

By separating emotion from logic and reason in the classroom, we've simplified school management and evaluation, but we've also then separated two sides of one coin—and lost something important in the process. It's impossible to separate emotion from the important activities of life. Don't even try.

Similarly, we've tended to think of a body/brain split: our brain regulating body functions, and our body providing support services to our brain. Scientists have now replaced this duality with an integrated body/brain system. Further, our brain, endocrine, and immune systems, long viewed as separate entities, are now seen as an integrated biochemical system. Our emotional system is located principally in our brain, immune, and endocrine systems, but it also affects such organs as our heart, lungs, stomach, and skin.

Think of our emotions as the glue that bonds the body/brain integration—and peptide molecules and emotion mechanisms as the physical manifestation of the bonding process. We could also imaginatively think of emotions as the glue that could help us make an integrated curriculum out of a curriculum composed of separate, logically defined disciplines.

School Practices

Although the educational applications of emotion research are still quite tentative, several general themes are emerging, and they tend to support an educational perspective that many educators have long advocated. This isn't surprising, because educators constantly interact with students' emotions—and so we do learn what works and what doesn't. What emotion research may provide for the first time, however, is scientific support for such beliefs. Six themes and broad curricular strokes follow:

Accepting and Controlling Our Emotions. Our emotions simply exist—in many cases as a survival mechanism that allows us to respond quickly and decisively before we have obtained all the relevant information. We don't *learn* emotions in the same way that we learn a telephone number, and we can't easily change them. What we can learn is how and when to use rational processes to override our emotions or to hold them in check—and when to allow them free reign as an exuberant manifestation of life. In an attempt to enhance institutional efficiency, schools have tended to rely on imposed control over students and staff. Instead, we should seek to help students and staff develop forms of self-control that encourage the nonjudgmental, nondisruptive (and perhaps even inefficient) venting of emotion that generally must occur before reason can take over. We all can recall incidents from years past that still anger us because our emotions weren't allowed free expression before a decision was imposed on us.

It's not difficult to move toward the inclusion of emotions in classroom life—for example, to simply draw a class into a tension-releasing circle after a playground fight and then play a game of circle tag before sitting down to talk out the problem. When the students' collective limbic systems have had their say, the slower-developing rational cortical processes can participate in settling the issue. And if that doesn't work, play another game or sing a song (as William Congreve suggested about 300 years before the scientific study of emotion began, "music hath charms to soothe the savage breast"). The point is to continue the dialogue, and accept and deal with the accompanying emotions when attempting to solve a problem.

Using Metacognitive Activities. Students know quite a bit about the complexity of emotions, and the personal way in which we experience them (Saarni and Harris 1989). Thus, schools should focus more on metacognitive activities that encourage students to talk about their emotions, to listen to the feelings of classmates, and to think about the motivations of people who enter into their curricular world. For example, the simple use of WHY in a question focuses the discussion toward motivations and emotions, and away from mere rational facts. *Why did the pioneers settle where the two rivers came together?* is a much more emotionally loaded question than *Where did the pioneers settle?*

Using Activities That Promote Social Interaction. The school activities that provide the most emotional support tend to emphasize nonevaluative social interaction (e.g., games discussions, field trips, interactive projects, cooperative learning) and engage the entire body/brain in the activity (e.g., phys ed, the arts). Although we've long known that such activities enhance students' enjoyment and learning, we still think of them as something special, as a reward, and so withdraw them when students misbehave. And, unbelievably, schools eliminate them as frills when the budget gets tight!

Using Activities That Provide Emotional Context. Memory is contextual, and the context of an experience often triggers emotion. The reoccurrence of the emotional state in which a memory was formed can thus trigger the recall of the memory. For example, fire drills are usually unannounced so that they produce an emotionally charged setting similar to the one students will have to deal with during a real fire. Such emotion-laden classroom activities as simulations, role playing, and cooperative projects can provide the important contextual memory prompts that a student may need in order to recall the information during a closely related event in the world outside the school. Doing worksheets in school prepares a student emotionally to do worksheets in life.

Avoiding Emotional Stress. Emotionally stressful school environments are counterproductive because they can reduce the students' ability to learn. A sense of self-esteem and control over one's environment are important elements in managing stress. Although highly evaluative and authoritarian school environments may promote such institutional values as economy, efficiency, and accountability, they may do so at the cost of increasing unproductive emotional stress in students and staff. It's often difficult to identify the fine line that separates intellectual challenge from emotional stress, but we must be aware of that line when dealing with the emotional lives of students.

Recognizing the Relationship Between Emotions and Health. Our emotions and our health are closely connected (Moyers 1993), but our profession hasn't really addressed the important relationship between a stimulating, emotionally positive classroom environment and the overall health of both students and staff. Health education should involve much more than the memorization of body parts. We need to think of students as more than just 100 pounds of brain tissue bobbing up and down in our classrooms.

John Dewey began this century with an eloquent plea for the education of the whole child. It would be good for us to get around to it by the end of the century—and emotion research may well be the catalyst we need.

Attention

Attention has always been a central concern of educators. Our brain's ability to focus and maintain its attention on objects and events is critical to learning and memory, and attention is a basic element in classroom motivation and management. Attention deficit disorder and dyslexia are two educationally significant attentional maladies.

Further, the design of our brain's attentional system suggests a curricular dilemma. The system evolved to quickly recognize and respond to sudden, dramatic changes that signal physical predatory danger, and to ignore or merely monitor the steady states, subtle differences, and gradual changes that don't carry a sense of immediate alarm. Schools, however, must now prepare students for a world in which many serious dangers are subtle and gradual—for instance, overpopulation, pollution, global warming, and acid rain. How do we reset a powerful cognitive system to meet these new challenges?

Until recently, cognitive scientists had only a limited understanding of our brain's attentional mechanisms and processes, so educators had to rely on their own practical knowledge of the system. That situation is changing dramatically as scientists unravel the mysteries of how and where our brain determines what to attend to, and what to merely monitor and ignore. Educators must understand the basic mechanisms and processes that regulate attention if we ever expect to make valid and useful applications of this research.

Brain Processes

An effective attentional system must be able to (1) quickly identify and focus on the most important items in a complex environment, (2) sustain attention on its focus while monitoring related information and ignoring other stimuli, (3) access memories that aren't currently active, but that could be relevant to the current focus, and (4) shift attention quickly when important new information arrives.

Some stable or innate elements in our attentional system develop early, and they automatically and predictably reduce the complexity of the surrounding sensory environment—and so allow us to respond quickly to sudden threatening events. Other more adaptable elements develop later, and we can teach these adaptable elements to respond to more subtle sensory stimulation, gradual changes, and social demands, such as school procedures (Ornstein and Ehrlich 1989).

Passive Beginnings. Attention generally begins as a passive process—the brief, unfocused reception of the multitude of molecules and rays that continually bombard our body's specialized sensory receptors with information about the outside environment. This period of passive reception is important because it allows our idling brain to process as many stimuli as possible while it actively searches for anything that might require immediate attention.

But because our brain can't process all of this information in detail, innate mechanisms limit the input to narrow ranges containing the potentially most useful information. The brain of each species is tuned to its specific needs. For example, our 10-octave sound range doesn't extend into the higher pitches that dogs hear, and visible light doesn't extend into the lower infrared levels that insects *see* but that we experience only as heat. Infrared light provides insects with information about flower petals and nectar sources that they need, but we don't.

Further, our innate attentional mechanisms are primed to focus automatically on information within those narrow ranges that contains high contrast or emotional intensity. Thus, even a passive glance will pick up rapid movements and the lines that define the edges of objects, and a familiar voice will automatically bound out of the babble and into our ears.[2]

Active Engagement. Passive reception quickly turns to active engagement as the sensory information moves through the brainstem[3] into two attentional processing systems: (1) the fast but limited emotional system, described earlier, that moves sensory information from receptors to thalamus to amygdala, and focuses on emotion-laden elements that might require a rapid response, and (2) a slower analytic system that moves sensory information from receptors to thalamus to sensory lobes to frontal lobes. Our frontal lobes play an especially important role in that they control, fixate, and shift our conscious attention—thus determining what's foreground and background, and how the current situation relates to our previous experience.

The focus and intensity of active attention can vary widely. Contrast a proofreader and a cursory reader of a magazine article.

The first carefully examines individual words and punctuation; the second focuses on the general content. When we consciously seek out such specific information, our attentional system primes itself in anticipation. It increases the response levels of all the networks that process that information, and it inhibits other networks. Thus the proofreader scans a page and spots spelling errors, and the cursory reader skims the same page and spots key content words and phrases.

In this active search for information, our brain frequently shifts its focus between external events and internal memories and interests. For example, while I'm listening to a friend's story, the memory of a related personal experience may suddenly pop into my mind. I'll usually shift my attention to my own mental story and merely monitor my friend's story while I'm processing mine. This attentional shift helps to maintain and update long-term memories by tying past experiences to the current situation. Much of our conscious activity involves the deliberate search for and attention to experiences that we know will trigger memories. Chapter 5 explores this process in more detail.

Focusing. Our principal attentional activity is the constant conscious selection of a current focus. We must extract what's most important from its context, and then focus on it while we monitor the context. Accidents resulting from attentional lapses, such as backing our car into a visible post, are a constant reminder that we have yet to achieve perfection in attending to the important and ignoring the unimportant. Emotion obviously dominates reason in many attentional decisions, and a stressful situation can chemically trigger an intense focus on something unimportant—such as when we work on an unimportant task to avoid facing a looming deadline on an important project.

Fortunately, our attentional system provides us with a short-term memory buffer that allows us to hold a few units of information for several minutes while we determine whether to go on to something else or store the data in our long-term memory. The advantage of this limited capacity is that it forces us to constantly select a relatively small focus of attention from a large (and often confusing) sensory field. The disadvantage is that it contributes to our human tendency to make inappropriate snap judgments.

Processing Complex Information. Our brain is designed to simultaneously process information from at least two noncompeting stimuli or from different dimensions within the same modality. We can simultaneously observe a friend's face, listen to her talk, and reach for our car keys; but we can't read a novel and write a letter at the same time. We can also increase our ability to divide our attention in some areas. Young children can't carry on a conversation while putting on a coat, but most older children can. An experienced teacher can monitor the specific behavior of more students than a beginning teacher can.

Conceptual development increases our attentional span by combining related elements into a unit (a process called chunking). From infancy, we automatically perceive a face as a unit (rather than as individual eye, ear, nose, and mouth elements), but beginning readers generally focus on individual letters and words and only gradually learn to read entire phrases as units. The intuition we ascribe to experts in a field may reside in their ability to rapidly size up a situation by identifying relationships and patterns among elements that novices don't recognize.

The Biochemistry of Attention. Our ability to maintain attention is affected by normal cyclical fluctuations in the efficacy of the neurotransmitter molecules that chemically regulate attention.[4] These fluctuations occur in 90-minute cycles across the 24 hours (Hobson 1989). People differ in their rhythmic patterns, but at about 6 a.m. many people experience a sharp rise in the availability of these attentional molecules (which causes us to wake up), and the average level of the molecules remains relatively high during the morning. The average levels begin to decline during the afternoon, and reach their lowest levels after midnight, when sleep becomes almost inevitable.

Unexplained curiosities abound—for example, our tendency to doze off around 3 p.m., when we should be awake, and to wake up at 3 a.m., when we should be asleep. Generally, however, we follow our body's predictable rhythms. We tend to do the things that we *have* to do during the morning, when it's easiest to maintain attention—and the things that we *want* to do in the late afternoon and evening, when it's more difficult to maintain attention without the emotional support of personal interest.[5]

Dysfunctions in Attention. Dysfunctional brain mechanisms and chemical imbalances can lead to attention deficit disorder (ADD) and other attention-related problems, such as retardation and schizophrenia. Although only a small percentage of students suffer from the form of ADD called hyperactivity (attention deficit hyperactivity disorder, or ADHD), their unfocused, restless, and impulsive behavior is very disruptive in the classroom.

ADHD probably emerges at least partly from lower metabolic activity and specific neurotransmitter deficiencies in brainstem and limbic system structures that (1) regulate motor inhibition and control and (2) project into the areas of the frontal lobes that organize and regulate goal-directed attentive behavior.

Properly prescribed stimulant drugs (such as Ritalin) that increase the availability and activity of such neurotransmitters as serotonin, norepinephrine, and dopamine seem to inhibit distracting stimuli and impulsive behavior, and thus improve the student's ability to attend to appropriate stimuli—to separate foreground from background information and attend to the foreground. The diagnosis and treatment of ADD is still a controversial matter, however, because of the side effects of prescribed drugs on some children.[6]

Dyslexia is another serious attentional problem that we treat with limited success. Livingstone and others (1991) have found that dyslexia may be at least partly a result of a coordination problem in the timing of the fast and slow visual pathway systems. Normally, the fast system processes the background (where objects are located), and the slower system processes the foreground (what the objects are). In people with dyslexia, however, the fast system appears to be sluggish; it doesn't erase the previous fixation quickly enough when the eyes move rapidly from word to word in reading, resulting in blurred and fused words. Lenses that absorb certain light frequencies may be able to improve the coordination, but scientists don't know for sure. Similar patterns of sluggishness may cause some auditory attentional problems (Galaburda 1993).

School Practices

Two guiding principles for classroom management and instruction emerge out of our current knowledge about attention mechanisms and processes. First, teachers should adapt their instruction to the built-in biases of their students' stable (or innate) attentional mechanisms. Second, they should use imaginative teaching and management strategies to enhance the development of their students' adaptable attention processes.

The Stable Mechanisms. Even though the scientific understanding of our attentional system emerged only recently, successful teachers have long grasped the first principle at the practical level. For example, most learn early to do such things as flip the light switch off and on to get their students' attention (because a voice command carries little contrast in a noisy classroom) and to follow repetitive sedentary work with enjoyable activities requiring more mental and physical energy (because interest and pleasure can activate a depressed attentional system).

A more intriguing example of teachers' intuitive grasp of the first principle is the tendency of elementary teachers to schedule individualized skill subjects in the morning and less precise, more socially engaging subjects in the afternoon (PE, art, group projects). It makes sense to schedule interesting activities that demand less precision and sustained attention in the afternoon, when students' inherent interest in the activity will elevate their chemically lower attention level.

While our attentional system has a built-in bias for high contrast, novelty, and emotional overtones, the curriculum presents a predictable universe: C-A-T always spells *cat*, and 6 times 5 always equals 30. We want students to solve such problems automatically and unemotionally—to achieve mastery—but mastery reduces students' need to actively attend to a process. It's a dilemma: the effective teaching of skills can reduce students' active attention to the process. Moreover, routine, low-contrast curricular tasks tend to bore students who spend hours with video games and TV programs, which too often emphasize the bizarre and violent—high-contrast behaviors that attract active attention.

Again, teachers have creatively responded at the practical level by adopting new (and, likewise, somewhat bizarre and violent) instructional methods: offering skill mastery games and scolding inattentive students are both ways of artificially increasing students' attention in otherwise unemotional, low-contrast learning tasks. For example, a math relay game is an active and fun-filled complement to the tedious task of mastering the multiplication tables. Such games artificially enhance attention-getting excitement through rapid action, and teachers have intuitively used them to adapt their instruction to the processing realities of their students' stable attentional mechanisms.

The Adaptable Processes. Our profession's principal challenge is to help students learn how to consciously manage the adaptable aspects of their attentional system, those that aren't preprogrammed to enhance human survival. Contemporary human life is more than attending to immediate survival. It is now vital that we humans also attend to the quality of our lives and to the potential gradual erosion of that quality.

Our attentional system constantly separates foreground from background, and focuses on the foreground. If we don't consciously control the decision about what's important, the system will revert to survival needs—and we'll end up trampling the beautiful flowers at our feet in a mad dash toward survival. It's important that we teach students how to ignore an insensitive comment that wasn't meant to hurt, how to develop into adults who can appreciate a work of art without asking its cost, how to simply observe a sunset.

The energy released by the plants surrounding a rocket launch site is at least as socially meaningful as the energy used to launch the rocket. Although we automatically attend to the televised blast-off, we have to learn how to attend to the equally important gentle growth of the plants in the background of the televised sequence. That's our curricular challenge.

A brain that can't control its own attentional system can be manipulated into thinking that background is foreground. Recent political campaigns have used shrill slogans to force limited but very emotional issues into the foreground, in order to meld more pressing and complicated regional and national problems into the background. The electorate and the media, focusing on their own survival, consistently fail to rise up in righteous anger to demand that the candidates reverse the attentional focus.[7]

The Classroom as Laboratory. Helping students attend to potentially important subtle differences and gradual changes is not an insurmountable challenge. Educators have already developed many practical responses to an attentional system we don't understand. We can expand effectively on what we already know and do. It's mostly a matter of emphasis.

Graphing can teach students how to identify gradual trends. Multicultural programs can celebrate both the unity of the human race and its subtle differences. History can explain how the past gradually became the present. Drama can demonstrate how a simple gesture can communicate what would otherwise take a page of script. And literature can allow us to look behind social facades.

Discussions, debates, and storytelling activities force students to hold bits of information in their mind so that they can communicate with others on the same subject. Cooperative learning activities oblige students to attend to others' contributions as well as their own. Simulations, role playing, and games require students to compare the real world with a created world. Metaphoric stories and dramas provide only the outlines of the story, forcing students to fill in the details. And metacognitive discussions about attention compel students to confront their own thought processes.

The bright, busy classroom environment we've developed, with its 20^+ students and continuous flow of sensory information, forces students to constantly make foreground and background decisions, to attend and respond to events outside and inside their skull. We can use the classroom as a laboratory for student attention research. Good, simple ideas will easily emerge in an exploratory environment. For example, a teacher may seek classroom analogies to larger population and pollution problems, and then ask the class to study and discuss them: the gradual build-up of classroom litter, the erosion of privacy in the group, the impact of hostile comments, the shifts in relationships. Before students can help to solve such problems in the larger world, they must learn how to solve them in their limited world.

Simple activities like these don't ensure a world solution to global warming and industrial pollution, but they do help students begin the process of attending to subtle differences and gradual changes. They help to reset our brain from its current built-in focus on the attentional problems of immediate survival to the subtler problems of the present and the foreseeable future. It's a beginning, and attention is a process that celebrates beginnings.

This chapter began with the premise that emotion drives attention, which drives learning and memory. Emotion and attention have been ill-understood gateways to learning and memory, which have always been the central focus of most of what we do in school. By understanding and then correctly using the power that emotion and attention can bring to learning and memory, we can materially increase the effectiveness of schools.

HOW OUR BRAIN
LEARNS, REMEMBERS,
AND FORGETS

If you want to know what water is, don't ask a fish. And if you want to know what memory is, don't ask a memory researcher—at least that's what memory researchers themselves believed until only recently. Indeed, after 30 years of intense study, the noted pioneer memory researcher Karl Lashley wrote somewhat wryly in 1950, "In reviewing the evidence on the localization of the memory trace, I sometimes feel that the necessary conclusion is that learning is just not possible." And only a dozen years ago, Neisser (1982) concluded that years of extensive psychological research studies have led to major generalizations about memory that the average middle-class American 3rd grader already knows through personal experience. Apparently, memory is so integral to our existence that we have trouble isolating it in order to learn what it is and how it works.

That situation is rapidly and dramatically changing. Brain-imaging technology can now clearly identify the brain areas that activate when a subject remembers or responds to something. For example, researchers have monitored the brain activity of subjects who have been asked to respond to nouns with the first verb that comes to mind (e.g., *cup* might suggest *drink*). A brain-imaging machine locates and reports the brain areas where the nouns and their related verbs are processed (Posner and Raichle 1994). Such research findings will help to resolve Lashley's lament of 45 years ago.

Other researchers have studied memory at the cellular level and, as Chapter 2 reported, much of this research has been done with simple marine snails. Scientists discovered that when an animal learns something, physical changes occur in the synapses of the network of neurons that process the memory, in effect strengthening the neural connections that constitute a memory network.

This cellular research required the development of technologies that could identify small changes in the structure of a neuron during memory formation. Since thousands of neurons can fit in a space the size of a pinhead, it's not surprising that such complex technologies didn't emerge until very recently. Historically, major developments in research technologies have sparked dramatic increases in our knowledge of various phenomena. Memory scientists are riding the latest technological wave, and they are rapidly moving from centuries of speculation to spectacular discoveries.

This chapter will focus on three elements of memory: (1) the physical changes that occur in neural networks when a memory is formed or erased, (2) the functional organization and operation of the several memory systems our brain uses, and (3) the procedures we use to maintain selected important memories.

Memory at the Cellular and Network Levels

Memory networks form their chemical connections at the synapse, the narrow gap that neurotransmitters cross when they move from the axon terminal of a presynaptic neuron to attach to receptors on the dendrites or cell body of a postsynaptic neuron.

When our sensory system focuses on an object or event, it activates a large number of neurons that are assembled into a variety of related brain networks (generally, combinations of columns). Each network processes a specific property of the object or event, such as its shape or movement pattern. This initial simultaneous activation creates synchronized response patterns in the coalition of activated neural networks—principally in their firing rates and in the amounts of neurotransmitters their neurons release. This ac-

tivity somehow links the networks that process the various properties of the object or event, and we get a mental impression of spatial integration—for instance, we perceive a face as a unit—even
though the various brain areas are operating independently, and no
single brain site contains the total face. Scientists don't completely
understand the process, but they believe that attention, thought,
and memory emerge out of such synchronized patterns of neural
network activity.

This activity is emergent because, for example, someone entering your classroom will perceptually cause a few key networks
governing shape, texture, color, and movement to fire rapidly and
rhythmically enough to quickly identify a moving human being.
This limited initial activity causes other memory networks that
deal with related information to fire in a similar rhythmic pattern.
These networks may provide more information: the stranger is a
female—about the same age as your students—with a bewildered
look on her face. Networks dealing with abstractions may also activate—for instance, seeing a religious symbol on the girl's clothing
may activate thoughts related to her value system. Thus, thought
emerges out of attention when a continuous, quite active, synchronized firing pattern resonates between a critical mass of related
neural networks in the thalamus (which processes the immediate
situation) and the cortex (which contains memories related to objects and events in the immediate situation). When enough information emerges about the immediate situation and about related
past experiences, a motor response often forms—in this example,
perhaps to move toward the girl in greeting.

A long-term memory begins to develop out of such a temporary
event when our brain determines that the event is emotionally
loaded and may reoccur. Suppose that the girl is a new student
assigned to your classroom. The same sets of neural networks that
initially represented the shapes that make up her face and body
will fire every time you see her because these shapes don't change
much from day to day.

The frequent activation of such interrelated networks and the
emotional realization that she'll be your student for some time will
eventually spark a pattern of similar physical changes that will
strengthen the synaptic connections of all the neurons in the relevant networks. One such change is the development of small
spines on the dendrites of postsynaptic neurons. This change in-

creases the number of receptors and allows more presynaptic neurotransmitters to attach to the postsynaptic neurons. Because a receiving neuron fires when the influx of information contained in neurotransmitters reaches the neuron's firing threshold, a presynaptic neuron that sends in a lot of neurotransmitter information will have more influence on the firing pattern of the receiving neuron than will a neuron that sends in less information. Adding receptors to a synapse increases the likelihood that the receiving neuron will quickly reach its threshold and fire (just as raising the thermostat setting a few degrees during the winter increases the likelihood that the furnace will turn on to heat the room).

Experience supports this theory: it doesn't take much input to trigger a strong memory, but it may take a lot of mental activity to activate a weak memory. When you enter a room containing a dozen strangers and acquaintances and a couple of close friends, your friends will *pop out* of the total group in instant recognition, because the networks that represent them activate more easily than the networks that process strangers and mere acquaintances— thanks to strengthened synaptic connections. Further, the complex changes that created the total memory of your new student activate her memory as a unit in rapid recognition of her when any part of the network is activated. For example, her face will instantly pop up in your mind when you see her from the back or when you hear her voice without seeing her.

As suggested in Chapter 2, an individual neuron can be part of many memories, much as a light bulb in an advertising reader board can light up as a part of many different letters, digits, and words. Thus, our relatively small brain can process a vast number of related memories. Further, our emotions connect memory networks to other related networks. When one network fires, it can activate other related networks. A visit to your childhood home will activate the memory of many events and objects that you hadn't thought of in years.

Memories are composed of constant and changing elements that vary in their ease of recall. For example, the shape of your student's face would remain constant over the year, but the clothing she wears would change from day to day. Your brain would thus create a much stronger memory of her constant elements than of her changing elements, and so you would easily recognize her face a year later. You might remember the *kinds* of clothing she tended to wear, but you would have difficulty remembering what she wore on any given day when she was a student in your class, unless it was something unusual that could create a strong memory after one experience.

Chapter 2 proposed a functional library model of our brain that located memories within interconnected cortical columns, much as a library book and its bibliography contain interconnected cultural memories. Would that things were so simple. Rose (1993) cautions us that although similarities do exist in how machines (books, tapes, films) and brains store and retrieve information, technological and biological memories aren't really the same. Technological memories are localized and static, while biological memories are distributed and dynamic. Moreover, a book requires an external reader's brain to retrieve its information; a brain retrieves its own memories to enhance both its survival and the quality of its life, two concerns irrelevant to a machine. So use the book model if you wish, but with the caution that models are simplifications of complex phenomena. Brains write books, but books don't develop brains.

Consider taped information. When musicians tape a song, their playing alters the magnetic properties of the tape, and so they've stored the musical information in a form of memory. But we need a tape deck, tuner, and loudspeaker to retrieve and use that *memory* information. The situation is similar with biological memory. The information stored via synaptic changes in neural networks (the memory engram) is only a small part of a much larger system that involves such processes as perception and emotion, synthesis and analysis, speech and writing. Memory is a function of the entire system, not just the synaptic changes. Further, the taped information sounds the same every time it's played on the recorder, but the musicians who taped the song alter their performance somewhat every time they play the song that's in their biological memory. Human memory is thus less precise than machine memory, and it is more adaptive and inventive over time as experience adds depth and breadth to the variability of our memories. Unfortunately much of our school testing program requires our students' very inventive biological memory system to exhibit high-level technological precision.

The Functional Organization and Operation of Our Memory Systems

Our memory system is functionally organized much like an office that must process a continual influx of information that competes for attention. We quickly label some information irrelevant and discard it. Other information we handle immediately and then forget about it. We set aside information to handle later, store some in permanent files containing related information, and incorporate some into the existing procedures for operating the office. Our brain has several interrelated types of memory systems that correspond to these general categories of information processing:

Short-Term Memory

Short-term memory is an initial memory buffer that allows us to hold a few units of information that we're attending to for a short period of time while we determine their importance. We must decide quickly because the continual influx of new information into our brain will delete anything not consciously held. This limited attentional capacity has important survival value in that it permits us to completely experience the current situation without having to remember any of it, and thus to quickly shift our attention to emerging situations that may be important. Luria (1968) described the terrible plight of a man without short-term memory, who remembered almost everything that ever happened to him. Imagine a complete lifetime memory of every boring party conversation you've ever had!

We've all experienced the fragility of short-term memory—just think of those times you've looked up a phone number and then instantly forgot it when someone interrupted with a question before you could dial it. The short-term memory process appears to function through temporary synchronized firing patterns that emerge between related networks in the thalamus (the current situation) and the cortex (related memories). The more rapidly firing, synchronized thalamus-cortex networks become foreground (attentional) information, and the less active neural networks become background (or context).

Because short-term memory space is limited to perhaps a half-dozen units of foreground information at any one time, we must rapidly combine (or chunk) related bits of foreground information into larger units by identifying similarities, differences, and patterns that can simplify and consolidate an otherwise confusing sensory field. Thus, we see a face as a unit, not as individual eyes, ears, nose, mouth, hair, and cheeks. This need to respond quickly has enhanced our ability to conceptualize and estimate, certainly major brain strengths.

Our conscious brain thus monitors the total sensory field while it simultaneously searches for and focuses on familiar, interesting, and important elements—separating foreground from background. Extensive experience in a field develops these rapid editing skills to the expert level. The curriculum enhances this remarkable brain capability when it focuses on the development of classification and language skills that force students to quickly identify the most important elements in a large unit of information.

The strong appeal of computerized video games may well lie in their lack of explicit directions to the players, who suddenly find themselves in complex electronic environments that challenge them to quickly identify and act on rapidly changing elements that may or may not be important. Failure usually sends the player back to the beginning, and success brings a more complex and attractive challenge in the next electronic environment. Contrast such an experience with the paper worksheets students receive in schools, which usually have clearly stated directions and static and uncomplicated information—but little cognitive challenge.

Students need many opportunities to develop their short-term memory capabilities through experiences such as debates and games that require them to rapidly analyze complex information and briefly hold key points in their memory. Flowing games, such as soccer and basketball, also have this continuous challenge. When textbooks and teachers highlight all the important information and when software is too user-friendly, instruction perhaps becomes more efficient, but students are deprived of the challenge and pleasure involved in continuously separating foreground from background.

Long-Term Memory

The development of a long-term memory emerges out of an ill-understood, often conscious decision that elements of the current situation are emotionally significant and will probably reoccur. If the situation does indeed reoccur after the memory is formed, sensory and perceptual processes will represent it in the thalamus. The cortical memory of the previous experience, resonating with the current thalamic perception, will then create an attentional state, and help to determine the response—current behavior influenced by past experience. Short-term memory allows us to experience the present, but we would become a prisoner of the present without our two interrelated forms of long-term memory, declarative (or explicit) and procedural (or implicit).

Declarative long-term memories are factual label-and-location memories—knowing the name of my computer and where it's located, for example. They define named categories, and so are verbal and conscious. The principal brain mechanisms involved in processing declarative memories are the hippocampus (in the limbic system) and the cortex (especially the temporal lobes). In library terms, think of the hippocampus as the card catalog that organizes the collection, and the cortex as the library's collection of books.

Episodic declarative memories are very personal—intimately tied to a specific episode or context (my first attempt to run my computer, my joy at discovering how it simplified writing and editing).

Semantic declarative memories are more abstract—context-free and often represented by symbols, such as those used in language and mathematics. They can be used in many different settings and so are important in teaching for transfer (knowing how to use function keys and software). My semantic understanding of the typewriter and its keyboard simplified my moves from manual typewriter to electric typewriter to word processor.

Initial skill learning, such as learning to type, is often episodic—the memories contain both foreground and background elements of the experience. When I learned to type, my teacher, classroom, and typewriter provided an important, easily remembered emotional context during the initial learning period. It would have been inefficient for me to continue to recall all these background elements whenever I typed, however, and so my teacher used class and home drills and different typewriters to help me eliminate the context of the learning (background) from the execution of the skill (foreground).

My typing knowledge and skill had thus become more semantic—more abstract, but also more useful in a wide variety of keyboard settings and tasks (background). In effect, my brain erased the background information from my memory by reducing its frequency and significance, and strengthened the foreground information (actual typing) by focusing on it.

My typing speed was limited, however, by my simultaneous conscious spelling of words and activation of keys, and so I also had to eliminate this conscious behavior through a transfer of skills from semantic declarative memory to procedural memory—to master automatic touch typing.

Procedural long-term memories are automatic skill sequences—knowing how to touch type, for example. Because they don't rely on conscious verbal recall (except to initiate, monitor, and stop the extended movement sequence), they are fast and efficient. They are also difficult to master and to forget (we can roller skate after years of not doing it) and are best developed through the observation of experts, frequent practice, and continual feedback. As a skill develops, the number of actions processed as a behavioral unit increases, and prerequisite skills are integrated into advanced skills. For example, learning to navigate a bicycle around the neighborhood during childhood enhances car-driving skills during our adult years.

The principal brain mechanisms involved in processing procedural memories are the amygdala (our brain's emotional center, located in the limbic system), the cerebellum (located in the lower back of our brain), and the autonomic nervous system (which regulates circulation and respiration)—but procedural memories also involve altered muscle systems.

At the survival level, the procedural system needs an emotional trigger (the amygdala) that can quickly activate the automatic motor system (the cerebellum) when enough threatening factors emerge, such as the sight and sounds of a rapidly approaching predator. It's advantageous for our running mechanisms to fire automatically, sequentially, and in loops (right foot, left foot, right foot, etc.) so that our conscious cognitive systems can focus on determining the best escape route. Thus, the procedural system is designed so that the motor neurons that process each action automatically trigger the next action in the sequence (think of a line of falling dominoes). What we've done over eons of time is to adapt the automatic neural machinery initially designed for running down food and escaping from predators to such contemporary activities as typing, speaking, driving cars, and playing piano passages.

When I was learning how to type I knew where all the keys were, and I was slow because my typing actions weren't connected into a complex automatic sequence. Today I don't consciously know where any of the keys are, and I'm a fast, efficient typist. My fingers have now become an automatic extension of my brain's language mechanisms.

We can easily move between conscious and unconscious activation of these processes. For example, suppose I decide to walk to a meeting. My initial steps will be conscious, but the process will quickly become automatic (procedural)—and I can then simultaneously walk and think about items on the meeting agenda. Were I to confront an obstruction, however, my walking would become more conscious as I moved around the obstruction, and I would temporarily stop thinking about the meeting because the two activities would have overloaded my conscious attentional brain processes.

Our brain is most efficient at recalling and using episodic memories that have important personal meanings. It is much less efficient at mastering the important context-free semantic and procedural memories. That's why schools have to spend so much time and energy on worksheet-type facts and skills that are isolated from specific contexts (but that generally have the important value of being useful in a wide variety of contexts). Conversely, computers, reference books, and so on are very reliable with facts and procedures, but they lack the emotional contexts that make our value-laden episodic memories so rich.

A memory is a neural representation of an object or event that occurs in a specific context, and emotionally important contexts can create powerful memories. When objects and events are registered by several senses (e.g., seeing, hearing, touching tasting), they can be stored in several interrelated memory networks. A memory stored in this way becomes more accessible and powerful than a memory stored in just one sensory area, because each sensory memory checks and extends the others.

Recognition is easier than recall because recognition occurs in the original context of the memory, or in one quite similar. If the emotional setting in which a memory originally occurred is tied to the memory, re-creating the original emotional setting enhances the recall of that memory and related memories. Thus, such emotional, multisensory school activities as games, role playing, simulations, and arts experiences can create powerful memories.

Procedural memories tend to govern the behavior of animals, whereas the much more flexible (easily learned, easily forgotten) declarative memory system is very important to humans. The combination of the two types of memory creates a powerful, integrated human memory system: thoughtful action.

The two systems appear to collaborate in such memory issues as the repressed memories of sexual abuse. Kandel (1994) suggests that the fearfulness of the abusive experience can lead to the release of norepinephrine (adrenaline), and this strengthens the amygdala-cerebellum connections that process the emotional memory of the event. Conversely, the painfulness of the experience can lead to the release of opiate endorphins that weaken the hippocampus-cortex connections that process the conscious memory of the factual circumstances surrounding the event.[1] Subsequently, the victim tends to avoid anything that triggers the fearful emotion, but doesn't consciously know why. This behavior makes sense. It would be important to avoid the person and the specific setting involved in the abuse, but if the person is someone whose support you need, and if the setting is your home, not remembering the details of the abuse may actually be a form of survival—a case of psychological escape when physical escape is difficult.

Years later, a chance combination of similar characters, location, actions, and emotions may be enough for the strong emotional memory to trigger the recall of the weak factual memory of the original circumstances of the abuse. Think of how the strong emotional and contextual overtones of a class reunion suddenly trigger the weak factual memories of many decades-old and seemingly forgotten school experiences.

Kandel cautions that this explanation of repressed memories doesn't ensure the truth of such a memory because the same neural structures that process perception also process our imagination. Thus, we can incorrectly believe that an imagined event is a real, perceived event.[2] A nightmare, which can often leave us trembling and sweating, is a common example of this kind of error.

Maintaining Our Memories

Why do we devote a third of our life to sleeping and dreaming, several hours a day to mass media, and much of the rest of our waking day to informal conversation and storytelling? Why do remembrances of previous experiences suddenly pop into our mind while we're listening to stories that other people tell? Why do parables and songs provide us such a rich lore of moral and ethical information? Why do our brightest students take the leading roles in classroom discussions?

A growing number of memory researchers believe that such activities are fundamental to the development, maintenance, editing, and retrieving of our long-term memories (Schank 1990, 1991). Although only limited research evidence supports this thesis, the basic idea has a ring of rightness about it that further research should confirm. For educators, the theories provide a fascinating new view of the role school activities play in the maturation of a child's brain.

Because the development of a long-term memory requires the physical reconstruction of the synapses in the affected neural networks, it is necessary to shut down their activity during the rebuilding process, much as a paving crew must detour traffic during the reconstruction of a road. Our brain does this through sleep (and perhaps during daytime periods of reduced activity in the relevant brain area). It reduces sensorimotor activity for about eight hours every night while it reconstructs and resets the memory networks that have emerged out of the day's events. Thus, sleep enhances the creation, editing, and erasing of memories.

How Dreaming Maintains Survival Memories

Memory networks must be constantly stimulated or else the neural synapses that were rebuilt to create an easily activated network will revert to their original state, and the memory network will disintegrate. We call this disintegration forgetting. Some researchers believe that dreaming helps to extend the life of important survival memories that aren't sufficiently activated during normal daytime activities (Hobson 1994) and to erase obsolete memories (Crick and Mitchison 1983).

Hobson (1989) discovered that every 90 minutes during a sleep period called REM sleep (rapid eye movement), certain brainstem structures begin to fire randomly into the cortex, where declarative memories are stored; it's as if sensory information is entering our brain when it isn't.[3] Whenever this random firing activates a memory network, however, what occurs in our mind is much like what occurs when we unexpectedly hear the word *banana*. We instantly see a banana in our mind, even though no banana is present. The sound memory of banana activated the sight memory of banana. Thus, during these four to five nightly dream periods (which range from 10 to 40 minutes in length), our brainstem constantly and randomly activates memory networks. It's somewhat like a circuit-testing and updating process for maintaining key survival programs so that they'll be functional when we need to use them.

Our mind assembles this random activity into the unconscious stories we call dreams—trying to make sense out of random nonsense. If the dream gets too emotionally intense (often around 3 a.m.), we wake up and end the dream. This two hours of nightly dreaming (more than 700 hours a year) maintains many of the important memories of things that don't occur often in real life (e.g., escaping from danger, remembering relatives who don't live nearby). The more connections a memory has to other memories, the more apt it is to be activated by this nightly random firing. The sexual and violent content of dreams tends to be high because our sexuality and survival are so closely tied to many aspects of our self—and so to many of our memories. Hobson (1994) reports that about two-thirds of our dreams are about unpleasant events—and so the parting expression "Pleasant dreams" has a hopeful meaning.

During REM sleep, our motor system is inhibited so that we don't act out our dreams. We commonly experience this phenomenon as running in sand while trying to escape danger. The cortex has sent a message to the motor system to run, but the motor inhibition stops the message prior to action.

Although dream periods allow animals to maintain the relatively few memories of survival strategies they must develop, we humans live in a much more complex social environment. We can't depend on random dreaming to maintain all the important memories that we develop.

What we appear to have done is to adapt the skill-sequencing efficiency of procedural memory to our need to recall the combinations and sequences of facts that form declarative memory. We've created a variety of *storytelling* formats that efficiently string together the related factual events of an experience. Recall that in a procedural memory, each action in a skill sequence automatically triggers the next action, and so simplifies recall. Stringing the separate events of a remembered extended factual experience into a logical sequence (such as the order in which vacation events occurred) places each subsequent event into the context of the previous event, and context enhances recall. Thus, it's much easier to use a narrative format to remember several events that occurred during an experience than to try to remember the events in isolation from each other. Just begin the story and let it logically and automatically unfold. The discussion below explores the basic storytelling formats we humans have developed to enhance the recall of declarative memories.

How the Mass Media Maintain Broad Cultural Memories

Metaphoric forms of mass media provide us with many narrative opportunities to consciously stimulate the memories we want to maintain. We go to a theater to see a film we believe will focus on something that's important to us. We get comfortable, the lights go down, conversation stops, and film images and sound magically appear. We soon find ourselves caught up in the events depicted on the screen, and personal memories related to the story suddenly pop into our mind.

So it is with novels, TV programs, songs, games, and pageants. We consciously seek out those that we hope will stimulate our memories of broad cultural issues that we consider important. It's like we're seeking out dream possibilities while we're awake. We tend to be unhappy with a mass media experience if we can't identify with any of the characters, locations, or events. Many people who watch professional sporting events are probably reliving their own adolescent participation in these games. They probably weren't nearly as good as the athletes they watch, but they can imagine that they were.

The most powerful metaphoric experiences are those that focus on important cultural issues, but define the story's characters and locations somewhat loosely, so that many people can easily identify with the issues the story explores. The parables that Jesus told are a good example. Many people learn these stories during childhood, but discover their deeper meanings as adults. Seeing a person in need or someone committing an altruistic act could spark the recall of the story of the good Samaritan, and over time many increasingly deeper connections could evolve between the parable itself and our life experiences.

Similarly, the songs of our adolescent years often become the beacons of our adult life because they help us to recall the important developments of our adolescence. We often listen to this music and flock to nostalgic concerts to relive the memories in the extended reverie of song. The song slows the simple message so that we can savor all the emotions of the experience.

How Conversation Maintains Informal Personal Memories

The mass media tend to focus on broad social concerns, but many of the memories we want to maintain are highly personal, and not apt to be turned into a novel or film. We maintain such memory networks informally through conversations with friends who shared the experience or who had similar experiences. Families get together on celebratory occasions that spark the recall of earlier celebrations. We'll converse with anyone who is willing to talk about a topic of mutual interest—each person's story or comment in turn sparking a contribution from the other person.

When we listen to another person's story and a related experience suddenly pops into our mind, we tend to quit listening to the other person's story and focus our thoughts on ours—and then we insert our story into the conversation at the first opportunity. Schank (1990) argues that we don't listen to the stories of others to learn about their experiences, but rather in the expectation that the interaction will enhance the maintenance of our own related memories. Conversely, we may opt out of an event, such as a class reunion, because of the high probability that it will spark painful memories. Further, a friend may decline to respond to our query about a recent negative event because she is trying not to create a story memory of it.

The value of a long-term relationship may reside in the constant availability of a storytelling partner who is willing to help recall mutually important events. The furnishings and art in a couple's home are historical artifacts that spark memories that define the relationship. The tragedy of the dissolution of such a relationship may well lie in the irreplaceable loss of the common history. The memories become vulnerable when the conversations cease. Conversely, a partnership may deliberately dissolve when the partners no longer want to listen to the other's version of events that were perceived and remembered differently.

How Schools Maintain Formal Societal Memories

Much of our culturally important information doesn't come up in dreams, in mass media, or during meal conversations—for example, the multiplication tables, how to spell *accommodate*, the names of countries and their capitals, how to compute the area of a circle. Our society has created schools to ensure that students master such culturally important information and then have opportunities to test their memories in simulated and real-life settings.

A school functions somewhat like daytime sleeping and dreaming. Recall that six hours (75 percent) of our nighttime focuses on the creation and editing of memory networks, and two hours (25 percent) involves dream periods in which the networks are randomly activated and organized into dream stories. This set-up sounds a lot like school. Teachers tend to focus more of their time and energy on teaching new information (i.e., creating memory networks) and less on using that knowledge in such social problem situations as discussions, games, simulations, role playing, storytelling, music, and art (i.e., circuit testing).

Further, students tend to view school as a somewhat surreal, random, dreamlike experience. Spelling follows arithmetic or vice versa; the teacher suddenly lashes out at a student; someone throws up; it's time to go to the library; it's anyone's guess whose hand will go up when the teacher asks a question, or even what question will be asked . . .

It is the student's task to make sense out of all this nonsense, to translate the seeming curricular randomness into a coherent view of our culture. Unfortunately, our culture seems to value random facts, and schools tend to reinforce this bias. For example, the students who score the highest on objective tests containing many discriminating items (items that elicit many incorrect responses) tend to be those with the best command of the most obscure facts—and obscure facts are almost by definition *unimportant* facts. The same holds true for the winners of TV quiz shows and games like Trivial Pursuit—some of us love to bounce random facts around in our mind.

Our task as educators, however, is to help students begin to find *relationships* between the somewhat random, often trivial fact-filled experiences of everyday life and the fewer enduring principles that define life—and then to help them create and constantly test the memory networks that solidify those relationships.

The memory theory and research presented in this chapter suggest that the best school vehicle for this search for relationships is storytelling as a broad concept that includes such elements as conversations, debates, role playing, simulations, songs, games, films, and novels. The brightest students are the ones who always have their hand in the air to expand the discussion through stories about their own experiences—to maintain and extend their own memory networks through active recall, as it were. It's as if their brains know how important it is for them to act on their knowledge and beliefs, to not sit passively and let their classmates make the mental connections.

We certainly can't rely on the random nature of dreams and the mass media to maintain our students' memories of socially important information. And it isn't enough for us to forcefully forge new memory networks in our students. We must constantly help students test their memories in real and metaphoric life settings that encourage stimulating interaction, or else all our efforts to create the memories are for naught. Watching a film doesn't help us maintain memory networks unless we become emotionally involved in its story; likewise, watching a teacher teach doesn't help students maintain their memory networks unless they, too, become emotionally involved in the exploration of the "story" at hand.

Bright students tend to have the mental ability to take a simple (even random) event and find relationships between it and some curricular issue. They thus can become a very useful classroom resource for beginning story lines and moving them along. But this can happen only in a classroom in which the teacher encourages the students to tell their stories to each other and to themselves.

How Our Brain Processes Our Stories

Schank (1990) suggests that the formation of a story about an experience is a memory process involving five stages that can reduce something like a two-week vacation trip to a relatively short, basic story that we effortlessly tell when someone asks us about the experience, and that we can adapt to the specific interests of different listeners:

1. Define the Gist. As we recall the total experience to create the memory, we distill all the separate events into the key elements that constitute the gist (or essence) of the experience. Over time, these elements may change as the experience becomes a more important event in our life, perhaps in ways that we didn't anticipate when the experience occurred.

2. Sequence the Activities. We arrange the events into a sequence that enhances the memory and the meaning, such as chronologically or in terms of importance. Each event triggers the memory of the next event in the logical sequence.

3. Index the Story. As we formulate our story, we index key concepts and terms in our memory that will allow us to easily recall the events that we plan to include in our story—and that will trigger memories when we listen to the stories that others tell. This is also what we do externally when we jot down notes for a lesson or presentation.

4. Tell the Story. We tend to use natural conversational language when we tell our story, and so we actually make up much of the story during its telling.

5. Amplify the Story. When we tell our story, we insert credible details that we didn't specifically store in our long-term memory of the event, but that we know occurred from our general knowledge of how the world normally functions (e.g., that the plane landed when we reached our destination).

Storytelling is a natural process that we generally don't consciously carry out (except perhaps when we formally plan a lesson or write out a story). It allows us to combine a complex combination of objects and events from our declarative memory storehouse into a sequential format that, in some ill-understood manner, enhances the memory of all of them. As suggested earlier, it's probably a declarative memory adaptation of the ancient skill sequences that constitute procedural memory. Our brain tends to adapt and recycle any efficient process.

Many things can't be communicated easily outside the context of a story—for instance, telling a family member what we did during the day requires us to at least list a sequence of events, which is the very framework of a story. And sometimes a story clarifies meaning for us in a way that facts or concise definitions cannot—when defining a word such as *chutzpah, weird,* or *insensitive,* for example, storytelling seems to work better than a dictionary definition because it creates many possible connections for remembering the meaning of the word.

Part of our brain's love of storytelling certainly lies in the challenges that stories often present to us. We enjoy figuring out the gist of a story, independent of the storyteller's explaining it to us. We tend to get angry if someone tells us how a film we plan to see turned out. We prefer to get the point of a joke on our own. We enjoy mystery stories, even though they follow a formula.

To be human is to be a storyteller. A computer can tell us how many words are in a story, correct some spelling errors, and execute other mechanical tasks—but it doesn't have a clue to what the story is about. Conversely, although children will miscount the words and miss many spelling errors, they can easily tell us the gist of the story—and even imaginatively recount the story in their own words. Perhaps our brain's affinity for storytelling explains why the humanities are so basic to education.

HOW OUR
BRAIN SOLVES
PROBLEMS

Only a relatively small number of our brain's tens of billions of neurons are directly involved in sensorimotor interactions with the environment, or with the regulation of basic body processes. Most of our brain's neural networks process the complex interactions that lead to the analysis and solution of problems. They interpret sensory information, compare it with related recalled information, and determine how best to respond to the environmental challenges we confront.

Our brain uses four basic problem-solving procedures that draw on its own biological resources, other people, technology, and drugs:

1. We solve most problems within our own body/brain. Some responses, such as removing a hand from a hot surface, are quick and unconsciously automatic; others, such as purchasing a home, occur only after much deliberate thought and planning.

2. Our social orientation encourages us to temporarily borrow the brains of others when we can't solve a problem by ourselves, such as when repairing our car or pleading our case in court.

3. Our brain has developed various forms of technology to solve biologically impossible problems and other difficulties. For

instance, telephones allow us to converse at great distances, and phone books eliminate the need to memorize hundreds of phone numbers.

4. Our brain has also discovered how to use herbal and synthesized drug molecules to temporarily alter its chemical composition and thus its normal behavior, such as staying awake when our attentional mechanisms would normally shut down, or falling asleep when our attentional mechanisms prefer to party.

This chapter will explain how our brain solves problems through its own resources and those of our environment. It will also suggest how to help students understand the nature of problem solving and make the best use of their brain's considerable problem-solving capabilities.

Solving Problems Biologically

Biological survival is obviously the most important problem that our brain confronts, and so we're typically born with fully functional circulatory, respiratory, and glandular systems. We also typically have access to adults who will carry us before we can walk, and provide food and shelter until we can independently take care of such needs. Independence in problem solving emerges during childhood and adolescence as our brain gradually matures and wires itself up to the problem-oriented environment in which it lives.

As discussed in Chapter 1, new brain theories argue that we're not born with an essentially blank brain shaped entirely by the environment. Rather, many key brain areas are already genetically dedicated to general human problems and their solutions, though they may not be functional at birth. The language areas, for example, are dedicated to processing language as a human function, but not to processing a specific language. Language emerged as an innate human capability long before any current language developed. Thus, the environment inserts the local language into the already dedicated general language areas of a child's brain.

In *Frames of Mind: The Theory of Multiple Intelligences*, Howard Gardner (1983) proposes that our brain is designed to process seven distinct forms of intelligence—innate cognitive capabilities that focus on important problem areas that our brain confronts.[1] He further argues that although these seven systems are highly inter-related, each system is also autonomous in that distinct brain areas are dedicated to processing its function.

The problems we confront in life contain important temporal, spatial, and personal elements—the *when* and *where* of the problem, and how it affects us and others. Consequently, our brain (and especially our cortex) evolved to effectively process the temporal and spatial factors in the problems we confront, and the brain areas dedicated to consciousness and emotion evolved to create our sense of *self* and its personal and social relationships to a problem.

We can thus arrange Gardner's seven forms of intelligence into three general categories that focus on the temporal, spatial, and personal elements of the problems we face.[2]

Time and Sequence

The three forms of intelligence in the general category of Time and Sequence all require the ability to rapidly and effectively process and communicate temporal and sequential information: to solve problems related to information flow and development, temporal analysis and synthesis, and situational cause and effect. At their core, these communicative forms of intelligence require the ability to recall the past, experience the present, and anticipate the future.

Linguistic Intelligence. As reported in Chapter 2, the phonemes and letters that constitute the primary units of spoken and written language are meaningless in themselves. Linguistic information is coded into the sequence of the units and the length of the chain, thus permitting our language to use fewer than 100 meaningless sounds and written symbols to efficiently process an incredible amount of meaningful information. Our brain's ability to very rapidly processes linguistic information enhances our ability to think through and discuss complex problems. The various forms of storytelling de-scribed in Chapter 5 provide a practical format for stringing together and recalling related objects and events that would otherwise lose their context and relatedness, and thus not be readily available for the efficient solution of problems that involve them.

Children tend to develop oral competence in language prior to written competence, and they must master an average of about ten new words a day to reach a high school senior's vocabulary of about 60,000 words. Our linguistic ability is a remarkable form of intelligence that in most people is centered in the left hemisphere. Two especially important interconnected structures in that part of the brain are *Wernicke's Area* in the temporal lobe, which links language and thought (word comprehension), and *Broca's Area* in the frontal lobe, which processes grammatical structures and word production. A bundle of nerve fibers called the *arcuate fasciculus* connects these two structures, and when it develops (at about age two), children begin to speak in sentences.

Musical Intelligence. Emotion is central to our being, and so communication must get beyond nouns and verbs to the feelings that give meaning to mere names and actions. Our language provides adjectives and adverbs that insert a variety of qualities into verbal communication, and great storytellers can evoke powerful emotions through words alone. But songs go far beyond words in their ability to insert emotion into communication.

The basic content of most songs is quite simple: *I like you* or *I dislike you*. In songs, we tend to *like* such things as lovers, family, God, country, holidays, seasons, and sports teams, and we *dislike* such things as war, unrequited love, unfaithful lovers, and bad times—all pretty basic emotional concepts. So if all George Frideric Handel wanted to say was "Hallelujah, for the Lord God Omnipotent reigneth!" why did it take him five minutes to say it? Songs often extend vowel sounds and repeat words and phrases, slowing the expression of the basic message. Musical elements such as melody, harmony, rhythm, and volume become part of the message. Thus, the *performance* of the Hallelujah Chorus exalts its relatively simple and straightforward message far beyond mere words, and many people who disagree with its religious message find themselves emotionally moved by the musical expression of it. That's the power of music.

Music doesn't even need words to communicate emotion. Symphony orchestras, jazz combos, and marching bands play dramatically different styles of music without lyrics, evoking a unique emotional response from each listener. Although every listener hears the same musical message, interpretations of it can differ significantly. Obviously, music is not a language in the same sense that English is a language; sequences or groups of notes do not have the precise meanings that sequences or groups of letters do. Still, most of us tend to recognize certain tonal sequences and chords as music, and consider others to be mere noise, so music does have a culturally related sense of sequence and grammar to it, albeit one very different from that for any written or spoken language.

It's possible that music was a precursor of language—a primal ability to recognize and respond to rhythms and tonal variations that eventually led to the greater complexities of language. When we humans went on to develop language, we may have kept music around because we liked the positive emotional overtones that it added to our life and discourse.

For most people, music processing is centered in the right hemisphere (though rhythm is one element of music processed in the left hemisphere). Birds process their songs in the left hemisphere, where we process language. If music was a precursor of human language, it's possible that most of our brain's musical functions shifted over to the right hemisphere when the complexities of language began to dominate our left hemisphere functions. Trained musicians often activate left hemisphere mechanisms while listening to music, probably because they are also analyzing the music. Most of us just turn on our right hemisphere and enjoy the music.[3]

Logical-Mathematical Intelligence. Although several areas of mathematics, such as geometry, are focused more on space than on time and sequence, logical-mathematical intelligence fits into this category because its basic processes and arithmetic symbols form a language that communicates sequential, quantitative information (123 isn't the same as 321), and because its forms of analysis also follow sequential thought patterns in which one thing leads to another in if-then and cause-effect thinking.

Children begin to count and classify objects quite early in life, usually with encouragement from their parents. School formalizes this play process and students move from informal, hands-on mathematics to symbolic representations on worksheets. Arithmetic becomes the language of numbers, and for many, alas, mathematics never gets much beyond that level. Arithmetic is only a small part of mathematics—for mathematicians, math is more like an art form that explores, celebrates, and communicates the many patterns that emerge in our study of the universe.

It's possible that the much-maligned computer games that continually condense and expand complex patterns of time and space, and require the player to quickly act on such transformations, will do more to help students develop logical-mathematical processes than our current cultural tendency to equate arithmetic with mathematics, and to consider computation as the school's principal means of developing logical-mathematical intelligence.

The wide cognitive spread of logical-mathematical processes is evident in our brain, where both hemispheres and especially the frontal lobes are involved in the various processes that constitute logic and mathematics.

Space and Place

The two forms of intelligence in the general category of Space and Place focus on our ability to understand the nature of space and our place in it. They deal with such concepts as here and there, stop and go, large and small, in and out, touch and ignore. Intelligent action in this category allows us to *navigate* effectively throughout our environment.

Spatial Intelligence. Spatial intelligence focuses on our visual and tactile ability to accurately perceive and act on objects and forms in our environment—to use artistic, architectural, and navigational processes to adapt and re-create elements of our environment. In most people, spatial intelligence is centered in the right hemisphere.

Art is the celebration of the ordinary. Vincent Van Gogh took an ordinary three-dimensional vase of sunflowers and redesigned it into an extraordinary two-dimensional painting that has given 100-year life and worldwide exposure to a bunch of cut flowers that otherwise would have wilted in a week. Similarly, such people as architects, clothing designers, cooks, and inventors use ordinary materials to shape extraordinary shelters, shoes, sandwiches, and silicon chips. We decorate ourselves and our environment. We enjoy the feel of various textures. We make extended trips to see specific ocean, mountain, prairie, and urban vistas.

Navigation is an important spatial skill that gets us from here to there. In navigating, our brain appears to use two strategies that are probably innate: reliance on geometric cues (maps) and reliance on landmarks (memory). Stereotypical male/female navigational differences have long sparked arguments, as couples hopelessly lost on a trip scorn each other's navigational strategy.

Consider the navigational problems that males and females in small hunter-gatherer communities faced thousands of years ago, when our brain reached its current size and basic processes emerged. The male hunters followed circuitous paths and each hunt differed, so landmarks weren't as useful to them as being geometrically attuned to the direction of the prey and the base camp. Conversely, women were gatherers who stayed near the base camp; for them, knowing and discussing the specific locations of continuing sources of plant food was more useful than just knowing the general direction and distance of them.

Males and females can effectively use both strategies today, but researchers suggest that when giving and receiving directions men generally prefer to consult a map, while women rely more on landmarks (Pool 1994). Males and females are equally successful in getting from here to there, despite any innate navigational differences, but they still often argue strategy during the trips they make together. That's okay. It makes life interesting.

Our brain likewise seems to divide the navigational task. Our left hemisphere typically processes verbal directions and the right hemisphere processes our inspection of a map depicting the route (Restack 1994a).

Bodily-Kinesthetic Intelligence. Our culture is fascinated by the excellent control that dancers and athletes have over their body movements, and that jugglers and watchmakers have over the objects they manipulate. Bodily-kinesthetic intelligence is frequently associated with other forms of intelligence—the music that emerges through a pianist's control of fingering, the baskets that are scored through a player's navigational and ball-handling skills, the insights into the human condition that a mime communicates through silent movements.

Fine control over body movements involves the development of procedural memories and muscular changes that free our conscious mind to focus on strategy. Whether we're talking about hunters from eons past and their skill at throwing spears, or contemporary quarterbacks and their skill at throwing footballs, we're describing a virtuoso mix of intelligent, conscious plans and unconscious procedures. Asked to differentiate between piano players and pianists, the noted pianist Vladimir Horowitz scoffed, "Anyone can play the correct notes."

Bodily-kinesthetic intelligence involves (1) the basal ganglia, several structures at the base of each hemisphere that coordinate the actions of the sensory and motor systems, (2) the amygdala, the limbic system structures that provide the emotional trigger for movements, (3) the motor cortex, narrow strips rising above the ears in each hemisphere that code movements and joint positions, and (4) the cerebellum, the bump at the lower back of our brain that coordinates and fine-tunes automatic movement patterns.

Personal and Social Awareness

Chapter 2 suggested that our brain must focus simultaneously on our internal needs and values and on our interactions with the outside world—and so it divides these tasks between our brain's two major interrelated systems, (1) the limbic system/brainstem complex, which looks inward, and (2) the cortex, which looks outward. The two forms of intelligence in the general category of Personal and Social Awareness focus on our sense of self—who we are and how we relate to other people.

Intrapersonal Intelligence. Socrates said, "Know thyself." That's still good advice, although it seems to take most of our lifetime to achieve a reasonable understanding of and comfort with who we are, and who we would like to be. Sadly, many people never achieve this level of understanding. The search frequently involves an exploratory childhood, a tumultuous adolescence, an achievement-oriented early adulthood, a second adolescence around 40, and a mellowing out as one moves toward retirement and into old age.

Intrapersonal intelligence requires conscious access to one's own emotions, a whole-brain phenomenon that is centered within the limbic system. To recognize and respond to immediate pain and pleasure is a very basic form of this intelligence. To be able to understand and discuss complex and conflicting feelings about a personal issue is an advanced form of this intelligence. Advanced intrapersonal intelligence doesn't generally emerge until adulthood, because it requires the maturation of the frontal lobes, especially the prefrontal cortex, which matures in late adolescence. These same structures are important in the development of interpersonal intelligence.

Interpersonal Intelligence. We are a social organism, dependent on others for many very important things in life. Thus, it's important to be able to distinguish among people and their complex emotions.

Children discover the social nature of life early, within their family structure. Their awareness grows as they move about the neighborhood and join such social agencies as churches and scouts. For most children, though, the school becomes the principal agency for developing social awareness and competence. A family structure is vertical—a sequence of different ages within one value system. A classroom structure is more horizontal—a couple of dozen students of similar ages plus one adult representative of Western Civilization. Each student comes from a unique family structure and value system. A classroom that capitalizes on the diversity of its students provides an excellent opportunity for students to compare their family values with those of other families, especially within cooperative learning and project-related activities. Even the misbehavior and arguments that are common to classroom life provide an excellent social laboratory for learning how to get along with others who differ in their values and social competence.

Home-schooled children miss many of these important opportunities. Like it or not, the children their parents don't want them to associate with in school will be their adult neighbors and co-workers. One wonders where and when the home-schooled children will master the social skills they will need in our diverse culture if their contacts with peers are limited to those with similar values. As adults, will these children thank their parents for removing them from classmates who could have become their friends and acquaintances? Home schooling is a legal option that parents ought to select only if insurmountable problems prevent their children from attending school.

The new brain theories suggest that a person's innate brain capabilities and childhood experiences combine to develop each form of intelligence to its basic functional level in problem solving. Adult experiences can further develop each form of intelligence.

Imagine that we could measure the level of each of the seven intelligences at birth and chart the result on a scale like the one in Figure 6.1. For example, suppose that Allen was born with long dexterous fingers, perfect pitch, the neural basis of a good memory, parents who enjoy violin music, and other factors important to musical performance. Allen would probably score high on the scale in music intelligence (at level A) and might become a fine violinist. Suppose that Bob was born at a lower level in each of those capabilities, and so would score lower on the music intelligence scale (at level B). He could move up the scale and, in time, also become a fine violinist, but probably only after much more training and effort than Allen, who had a head start in musical intelligence.

Figure 6.1
Human Intelligences

	Normal Range of Human Ability	
Form of Intelligence	low (handicapped)	high (genius)
Time/Sequence Linguistic		
Musical	_____ B _____	A _____
Logical-Mathematical		
Space/Place Spatial		
Bodily-Kinesthetic		
Personal/Social *Awareness* Intrapersonal		
Interpersonal		

Each of us theoretically begins life with innate brain properties that place us at some point along each intellectual scale, and those who score high initially on a given scale will find it much easier to become successful in that intelligence than those who score low. Those who score below the normal human range may never get beyond low normal, despite high interest and good instruction. Those whose innate capabilities place them well above the normal range may actually profit relatively little from formal instruction to develop that intelligence.

We are a complex of intelligences that range across the scale and provide multiple approaches to meeting the temporal, spatial, and personal challenges of our environment. Success in one intelligence does not guarantee success in another. For example, a person can be a very successful athlete (spatial, bodily-kinesthetic intelligences), but have little success with personal relationships—or the reverse.

One important educational issue to emerge out of Gardner's theory is whether schools should focus on increasing students' strengths (the intelligences in which they are already strong) or on shoring up their weaknesses. Ideally, the schools should do both, being especially diligent to shore up any serious weakness that would handicap the student in life, and also to encourage those who have exceptional abilities. But what should be the *principal* focus of the school with students who exhibit differences in the various forms of intelligence, but who are within the normal ability range in all of them? The cognitive sciences have no clear answer to that question. It's a political issue.

Still, imaginative teachers have always used multiple approaches to the curriculum in order to open as many cognitive doors as possible. They presented information to students via one intelligence and then challenged them to paraphrase it using another. They developed open-ended projects that encouraged students to explore multiple approaches to the problem. They encouraged students with different interests and abilities to work together. It has always been done. Gardner's focus on the complexity of intelligence has provided welcome scientific support for those who have long believed that our society subscribes to too narrow a view of intelligence.

During optimistic periods, our society tends to believe in the positive power of change, and so it supports schools and social programs that are dedicated to improving people and institutions. During gloomy, pessimistic periods, we tend to believe that things won't ever improve anyway, and so we withdraw our support from schools and social programs, saying they're "just a waste of our hard-earned tax money." We're now mired in a pessimistic period, complete with controversial books such as Herrnstein and Murray's (1994) *The Bell Curve*, which uses IQ correlational data to argue that innate intellectual differences exist among racial and ethnic groups.[4] The result of all of this current turmoil is that we tend to forget about the tremendous power of both individual learning and cooperative behavior in a diverse society.

Solving Problems Cooperatively

One practical solution to the issue of what to do about the ability differences that typically exist in our several forms of intelligence is that we became a cooperative species, assigning community tasks so that the group could benefit from the strengths of each individual. For example, the best spear thrower became the lead spear thrower in the hunting party, and the entire group ate better.

Conventional wisdom incorrectly sees the human race as principally competitive, probably because the mass media focus on such events as wars, competitive crimes, business acquisitions, and sports victories. The mass media focus on the dramatically unusual, not on the norm in human behavior, and so the *news* typically reports what's new and unusual—the distortions of normal human behavior.

The human race wouldn't have survived if it were principally and violently competitive. Our race became a dominant form of life because we tended to help, not kill, one another. If we consider Gardner's seven intelligences, we can easily see that much of our brain's capability is tied up in processing activities that are chiefly social and cooperative. It's difficult to think of linguistic, musical, and interpersonal intelligence out of the context of social and cooperative activity, and the other four forms of intelligence are likewise principally social in normal practice.

A complex division of labor thus evolved in human society. I'll raise the wheat; bakers will bake the bread; and truckers will bring it to your neighborhood store—if you'll educate our children. Our economic system operates with forms of money and credit that assume most people are honest in their transactions. Our religious and ethical organizations stress love and acceptance. A vast number of helping organizations depend on charitable contributions and volunteer effort.

Wars, assaults, child molesting, and cut-throat business practices aren't what the human race is about. They represent forms of human pathology, not the norm.

Consequently, one would expect schools to focus on the development of skills that are more definitive of our species, that encourage and enhance social and cooperative behaviors, especially since we educate students in group settings and assign them common problems. I have always thought it odd that traditional classroom design and procedures separate students, and that most learning is evaluated individually, even competitively. Trees have to stay in one place, remain silent, and compete for the sun's attention. In some classrooms, alas, similar expectations hold for students.

Conversely, I don't find it odd that many teachers have embraced the development of classroom procedures that encourage cooperative behaviors—from progressive education at the beginning of this century to cooperative learning at the end. Our patrons are understandably concerned about the personal success of their individual children, but many classroom teachers are just as concerned with an overall climate of positive class relationships and attainment. Educational policy is driven by our patrons's concerns, however, so those who focus on the individual student and those who focus on the group engage in a continual tug-of-war.

This is really not an either-or issue. We do solve many of our problems individually and competitively, and so the development of individual problem-solving skills and competitive success is important, but we also depend on the abilities of others, and so schools must help students to develop both individual and cooperative skills. We've made curricular adaptations to the dilemma, in that skill development activities tend to be individually driven, and class projects and discussions tend to focus on group behaviors. My feeling is that individual activity and evaluation continue to predominate in most classrooms, and that we're reasonably effective in this area. Thus, we need to consciously seek a better balance.

Lack of individual or competitive ability generally isn't what causes people to lose their adult jobs or destroy their marriages. These failures are more often a result of people's inability to work effectively with others. In our multicultural society, the school is the place where children from diverse backgrounds come together, and thus it is the best place for them to learn to work well with others. Schools must focus more on helping students learn skills of cooperation. It's reassuring to note the development of cooperative learning programs that provide practical techniques for both teachers and students.

Solving Problems Technologically

A single curious human brain or a cooperative combination of very intelligent brains can't make a detailed unaided examination of the inside of a cell or the outside surface of the moon. We therefore developed technologies that allow us to do things that are biologically impossible, or that we can do only with great effort. Technologies have narrowed the distance between what we can do and what we would like to do. They've become, in effect, a kind of *technological brain* on the outside of our skull that interacts with and extends the biological brain on the inside. Typewriters, telescopes, telephone books, and trigonometry are but four of the rich complex of information technologies that we've developed to expand our brain's ability to gather, process, interpret, and use information in the solution of problems.

Powerful portable computers are the most educationally significant technological development of the past quarter of a century. They've transformed information processing in our society, but not yet in schools, where the pencil still reigns supreme. Although electronic media dominate storytelling in our society, schools still tend to focus on book reviews, not on reviews of films and TV shows; and students usually write their stories rather than videotape them. Most schools are more than a few steps behind the technologies that almost define our culture in the 1990s.

Technologies have always emerged out of our body/brain's limitations, and the computer is an excellent example. Let's compare the capabilities and limitations of both to discover how to make the best use of both in school.

Our brain is currently much better than a computer at conceptualizing ambiguous problems—at identifying definitive and value-laden elements that it can incorporate into an acceptable general solution. Conversely, a computer is much better at rapidly, accurately, and effectively processing complex sequences of clearly defined facts and processes that would otherwise require a high level of sustained mental attention and precision.

Or, to state the difference in classroom terms, teaching is generally a delightful experience when we focus on activities that student brains enjoy doing and do well, such as exploring concepts, creating metaphors, estimating and predicting, cooperating on group tasks, and discussing moral or ethical issues. Conversely, teaching loses much of its luster when we force students to do things their brains don't enjoy doing and do poorly, such as reading textbooks that compress content, writing and rewriting reports, completing repetitive worksheets, and memorizing facts that they consider irrelevant.

The 3 R's curriculum has historically been driven by a cultural need for students to master written communication (which is based on recognizing the correct sequence of letters, digits, and words) and to remember selected events, dates, and locations (which usually are not part of the student's first-hand experience). This kind of learning requires solitary sustained attention and precision, qualities that help to define our brain's limitations. Before the development of powerful portable word processors and calculators, we had no technological alternative to doing our spelling and computation either mentally or with paper and pencil, and so spent a lot of time and effort in such mastery. Two examples: Spelling consumed the equivalent of several months of the first six years, because pencils have no spelling checkers that identify errors with the click of a key. Mastery of multiple-digit divisor problems, which rarely occur in normal life, occupied weeks of arithmetic time.

Schools should not be trying to force students to match the computer's skill in performing some of the more tedious tasks involved in mathematics, written language, and the organization of data. This doesn't mean that we shouldn't continue to teach arithmetic computation, for example. It's easier to master such basic facts as 3 x 4 in our mind than it is to depend on a calculator. On the other hand, for a problem such as 345 x 56, which we would traditionally compute with paper and pencil, a portable calculator is the better aid. For those who say, "But what if you don't have a calculator?" the appropriate answer is, "So what if you don't have paper and pencil?" In either situation, you would estimate the answer or borrow the technology, and a calculator is now readily available in almost any group setting.

Combining the two technologies in classroom instruction isn't difficult. For example, ask students first to mentally estimate the solution to computational problems (or to use paper and pencil), and then to use the calculator to check their estimates. Such an approach would improve students' ability to estimate (a brain strength), teach enough paper-and-pencil calculation so students can use it when necessary, and improve calculator skills.

We should concentrate more on developing our students' ability to quickly locate, estimate, organize, and interpret information, and we should teach them how to use the superior speed and accuracy of available information technologies whenever a complex problem requires an accurate solution. Hypercards, spread sheets, statistical programs, and spelling checkers are only a few examples of the rapidly developing software programs that can assist our imprecise brains in solving problems and communicating ideas with detailed accuracy.

Because these software programs eliminate problem-solving steps we formerly did mentally, it's legitimate to worry that students won't understand important intermediate steps in problems they solve via such software. It isn't enough to suggest that many people who drive cars don't understand the internal combustion engine. We must develop curricular programs that effectively explain the complete solution process, while simultaneously teaching the student how to use a computer to solve the problem.

What schools shouldn't continue to do is to pretend that computers and calculators are still fringe problem-solving elements in our culture. We won't return to the earlier world in which our brains used the increasingly complex and cumbersome printed collection of information our society had amassed. The computerization of information has moved our brain well beyond its normal range, speed, and power. In doing so, it has created a new set of societal problems related to the value of the gain in relation to the effort and cost. Are things worth doing simply because computers have the power to do them?

Stress and drug-related illnesses are part of the personal and social costs of educational and technological efforts to force our body/brain to function well beyond its normal capabilities— whether it be to require students to use paper and pencil to solve math problems they don't understand and consider irrelevant, or to require them to use an equally incomprehensible computer program.

Thus, the challenge in technological problem solving isn't merely to teach students how to use computers—how to touch type and navigate through files—but also to understand the nature of computerized information, and the social, political, and ethical issues that computers create.

Solving Problems with Drugs

Sticks were probably among the first tools that we humans used in our long ascent to the complex technologies that have greatly extended the capabilities of our body/brain. The leaves or fruit of the bush that supplied that stick may also have provided the first drugs. Then, as now, humans used drugs because they allow us to do things that we otherwise couldn't do as easily—or even at all.

Drugs have been an important part of human life for millennia, but until recently, we didn't know much about what they were or how they created their effects. Consequently, drugs took on a mystical character. People spoke of magic mushrooms and reefer madness. Wine was the nectar of the gods. Drugs were incorporated into religious ceremonies and holiday celebrations. Experiences with drugs were both exciting and fearful, helpful and destructive.

Educating Students About Drugs

Drug education programs emerged out of this general lack of understanding of the psychobiology of drugs, and so a strong moral tone dominated: don't use drugs because they're not nice. Schools spoke of having a Drug and Alcohol Program (as if alcohol was something other than a drug), or of having a Drug-Free Campus (as if the coffee pots and soda machines were completely free of drugs).

Our knowledge of the biochemistry of drugs and how they affect body/brain problem-solving processes has dramatically increased in recent years, and this knowledge leap suggests that drug education programs should now go beyond the moral overtones, behavioral responses, and end effects of drug use to a stronger focus on clear explanations of what drugs are and how they work. This recommendation will certainly rekindle the same argument used against sex education programs: if you teach students about sexuality (drugs), they will become sexually active (use drugs). Well, we've been teaching algebra to students for centuries and they don't rush out and do algebra.

The curriculum should provide students with useful information—what things are, how they function, how to use them effectively and ineffectively. Drugs involve a biochemical process that may have moral overtones. Thus, it's better to focus first on the biochemistry. (The following summary of what we know about psychoactive drugs expands on the information on drugs in Chapter 2 and Appendix B.)[5]

What We Know About Psychoactive Drugs

Neurotransmitter molecules produced within a sending neuron pass information from that neuron to another neuron at the *synapse*. The complementary shapes of the neurotransmitter and the receptor on the postsynaptic neuron allow them to bind (somewhat like a key and lock) and then to pass and receive information.

The synapse is an area of constant molecular activity that would be chaotic without its simple molecular binding system. Think of a hotel with many people constantly entering, leaving, and milling about. Key codes and shapes ensure the correct match of patrons to rooms. The front part of a key contains the room's *address* and the back part represents the *information*—the patron who can enter the room. Anyone who holds the key or its duplicate has access to the room.

Psychoactive drugs are herbal or synthetic molecules that sufficiently resemble the molecules involved in brain processes to attach to the appropriate receptors. A psychoactive drug molecule enters our brain and a synaptic area through the bloodstream. Like a duplicate key, it uses its similar shape and electronic properties to attach to a presynaptic or postsynaptic receptor, and to alter one of a variety of chemical actions that occur in a synapse. For example, it can mimic the communicative actions of a neurotransmitter that is normally released into the synapse; or it can alter the rate and quantity of transmitter release, the shape and number of receptors, the strength of the action, or the ability of the presynaptic neuron to reuse its neurotransmitters.

These actions of psychoactive drugs can positively or negatively affect normal brain activity. Because the shape and electronic properties of drugs mimic those of brain molecules, drugs can obviously have positive effects, as exemplified by the widespread and continued human use of potentially dangerous legal and illegal drugs. Further, drugs can stabilize the imbalances in neurotransmitter distribution experienced by many people (e.g., lithium stabilizes norepinephrine distribution patterns in people suffering from bipolar affective disorder, or manic-depression as it was formerly called).

Because drugs flood into the synapses of a brain area via the bloodstream rather than through the carefully regulated axon terminals of interrelated neurons, their heavy concentrations and unregulated movements in and out of synapses can also affect us negatively—within the immediate brain region, and in other parts of our brain/body. Thus, the caffeine that keeps us awake (and perhaps alive) during the final segment of a long, late drive home will also probably delay our desired sleep because the effects of caffeine persist for over three hours. The alcohol that initially releases our inhibitions in a social setting can trigger inappropriate behavior and uncoordinated movements if we drink enough to affect more of our brain, and it can also destroy neurons involved in memory circuitry. The morphine that reduces pain and enhances euphoria in addicts also reduces our brain's production of its own opiates, and so extends the addiction.

An antipsychotic drug that dampens an overactive area of dopamine circuitry, and so frees a person from the ravages of schizophrenia, can also affect other areas of the powerful, interrelated dopamine circuitry if the dosage isn't carefully controlled, and improper dosages can eventually lead to movement disorders associated with Parkinson's disease. Cocaine acts within the same dopamine circuitry. It blocks the reuse of the neurotransmitter, and thus depletes our brain's store of it. The result is a violent mood and behavior swing—a short period of euphoria followed by a longer period of depression, during which our brain replenishes its store of dopamine. Drug use can be a dangerous business.

So psychoactive drugs are both helpful and harmful, and almost always require a tradeoff. To maintain a life of good quality, our conscious brain must carefully control its drug selection and dosage, just as its unconscious partners in our skull and glands carefully control the production and distribution of neurotransmitters and hormones.

The brain mechanisms that respond to our environment's challenges mature during childhood and adolescence. Extensive drug use during this period can adversely affect this maturation, because drugs alter our brain's perception of and response to the environment. Thus, one drug may help keep us awake so we can complete a task by its deadline, but another drug could destroy maturing neural networks that are critical to that problem-solving task. Drugs aren't good or bad, per se. They are *chemical technologies* that positively and negatively affect the processing effectiveness of our biological brain. The better solution is to learn how to use our own biochemical resources to solve a problem, and to use drugs only when that assistance is essential to maintaining an acceptable quality of life.

Students need this kind of factual, nonmoralizing information so they can learn to make their own informed, conscious choices about what they do to their body and brain.

7

HOW OUR
BRAIN ADAPTS ITSELF
TO ITS ENVIRONMENT

Our brain's maximum capabilities were genetically determined by its need to respond quickly and effectively to crisis conditions rather than by its need to respond to normal life challenges. Furnaces are designed on the same principal: models are guaranteed to function well during the coldest weather in a specific area, not just the average weather.

The basic genetic developmental pattern for our brain is thus quite simple and straightforward: (1) create an initial excess of cells and connections among related areas—in effect, temporarily wire up everything to everything, (2) use emotion, experience, and learning to strengthen the useful connections, and then prune away the unused and inefficient, and (3) maintain enough synaptic flexibility (commonly called *plasticity*) to allow neural network connections to shift about throughout life as conditions change and new problem-solving challenges emerge.

Consequently, redundancy and alternate systems abound in our brain: two hemispheres, pairs of amygdala and hippocampi, several sensory systems with paired organs that respond to overlapping properties of the physical world, and complex neural systems that define and process multiple intelligences. Each such structure and system is itself powerful in the normal challenges it confronts, but these structures and systems can combine marvelously to solve very serious problems; to create new explanations, artifacts, and strategies; and to overcome terrible assaults.

The emerging brain theories discussed in Chapter 1 argue that innate factors play a more important role in determining our brain's capabilities than was previously believed. Conversely, our profession has historically and optimistically focused on nurturing factors that can increase our brain's capabilities. Both positions strongly suggest that children should choose their parents carefully—the former because of the genes that parents pass on, the latter because of the cultural environment that parents create. But both positions also recognize that neither nature nor nurture can exist without the other. It's like trying to determine which hand contributed most to the sound of hands clapping.

The major educational question to emerge out of recent brain theory and research is this: How much effect do environmental challenge and stimulation have on the general and specific capabilities and limitations of our students' brains? This chapter will first report on key animal and human research studies that focused on this issue. It will then begin the discussion of the broad educational implications of this research that I hope you will continue with your colleagues and patrons as you explore applications. To put it simply, should we fine-tune, overhaul, or revolutionize our current classroom pattern of instruction?

Brain Plasticity Studies with Animals

Marian Diamond (1988) is one of a number of researchers who have used rats in carefully controlled studies of the effects of environmental stimulation and deprivation on the development of the brain's cortex, the large sheet of neural tissue at the top of the brain that processes environmental interactions. Although most of a brain's lifetime supply of neurons are in place shortly after birth, many of the axon-dendrite connections that process cognitive information develop after birth, as a brain gradually adapts to its environment and makes itself the unique result of its own experience.

In the human brain, this postbirth development results in a weight increase from about one pound at birth, to two pounds at age one, to three pounds at late adolescent maturation. Herman Epstein (1978) found a postbirth brain development pattern of growth spurts and plateaus that relate to the stages of cognitive development that Piaget had earlier identified, without the biological correlate that Epstein found (Flavell 1963).[1]

Our brain continues to adapt its networks throughout adult life as it adds, edits, and erases memories and problem-solving strategies, but these processes don't result in a weight increase. Think of an analogous pattern in the making and shifting of interpersonal connections in our lives. When we first move into a neighborhood, we tend to check out area businesses and facilities before settling into the basic group we then normally patronize. If we live in the same residence for years, we may change many of these initial connections—job, stores, friends, memberships. Despite these shifts, our total number of relationships may remain relatively constant over the years—a favorite grocery store and service station, a dry cleaner, a couple of dozen friends, and so on.

Brain plasticity researchers study rats, whose overall mammalian brain development pattern resembles that of humans. The basic research design (with variations) compares the brains of rats that have lived in different environments for differing periods of time: (1) rats living alone in a small, unfurnished cage, (2) a group of 12 to 36 rats living together in a large laboratory cage that contains a regularly changed and stimulating collection of toys and other objects to explore, and (3) a group of rats living in a much larger outdoor, seminatural rat habitat. Most of the research has focused on conditions 1 and 2.

As one might expect, the researchers found that the best cortex development emerged from the social and environmental stimulation of the rat's natural habitat, followed by the enriched social cage, followed at a significantly lower level by the impoverished solitary environment.

The socially oriented seminatural and enriched laboratory settings produce a thicker and heavier cortex: larger neurons, more and better interneural connections, and a greater supply of glial support cells. These elements create a potentially better brain for learning and remembering, defined in rats by their ability to run mazes. Researchers consistently found the most effects in the occipital lobes (vision), but all cortical regions respond positively to enriched environments. The effects are similar, whether 12 or 36 rats live together in the 3' x 3' enriched laboratory environment. Although a brain's plasticity is greater during the early developmental period, researchers obtained enhanced effects throughout the rats' lifetime. Indeed, they found significant general cortical improvements after only a few days when they moved adult rats from an isolated cage to an enriched social environment.

Although the cortex has a remarkable ability to adapt successfully to different environments, it does have its limits. A brain may be unable to recover from the effects of serious environmental deprivation during a critical brain development period. For example, Hubel (1988) discovered that an otherwise normal cat was blinded for life in an eye that was covered for only a few days during a critical period of visual development. He also discovered that adult cats were unable to effectively process vertical or horizontal line segments if they were reared in an environment devoid of such lines.

It's probably safer to generalize from rats to mice than from rats to human beings. For example, a rat brain fills a thimble, while a human brain fills a three-pint container. The forebrain occupies 45 percent of a rat brain's mass, compared with 85 percent in humans; frontal lobes occupy about 5 percent of a rat's brain compared with 30 percent of the human brain; the cortex matures in about a month in a rat compared with about 18 years in a human brain.

Still, researchers expect to find related patterns of plasticity in humans when they develop the technology to monitor growth in specific areas of the human brain—with the differences between rats and humans probably occurring in location and degree of plasticity. Diamond and her colleagues (1985) compared Albert Einstein's preserved brain with the brains of normal people and discovered significantly more glial support cells in the *angular gyrus,* an important cortical area that integrates sensory data and processes conceptual and symbolic thought.

The research involving an enriched environment is important for educators, even with the caveats suggested above. All mammalian brains process information similarly, and the enrichment research indicates that the basic networks regulating a brain's interactions with its environment can maintain their plasticity and vigor throughout life if stimulated to do so. Because neurons thrive only in an environment that stimulates them to receive, store, and transmit information, the challenge to educators is simple: define, create, and maintain an emotionally and intellectually stimulating school environment and curriculum.

As we begin this process of exploring what to do and when to do it, it might be useful to pause briefly to consider how our culture normally apportions the approximately 150,000 hours of living we expend between ages 1 and 18.

We sleep about 50,000 hours of this time, and we dream about two of the eight hours we sleep each night. As reported in Chapter 5, sleeping and dreaming appear to be positively related to the development and maintenance of *survival memories* and other long-term memories.

We spend about 65,000 of our waking hours involved in solitary activities and direct, informal relationships with family and friends, and these play a major role in the maintenance of *personal memories*.

We spend about 35,000 of our waking hours with our larger culture in formal and informal metaphoric and symbolic activities—about 12,000 hours in school and nearly twice that amount with various forms of mass media (e.g., TV, films, music, sports, print media unrelated to school). Mass media and school thus play major roles in the development of important *cultural memories*.

From this information we can see that on an average developmental day between the ages of 1 and 18, a young person sleeps eight hours; spends ten waking hours with self, family, and friends; four hours with mass media; and only two hours in a classroom-oriented school. Our society has incredible expectations for those two hours!

We can think of the traditional classroom as an artificial environment, somewhat analogous to the laboratory environments in Diamond's plasticity studies. Although critics argue that a school lacks the direct, stimulating challenge of the natural world, our society considers school a flawed but efficient way to deal with complex cultural information that doesn't generally come up in family life or the mass media. Further, the time apportionment reported above suggests that more than 80 percent of the waking hours of a child and adolescent are spent outside of school in family, peer, and electronic environments that range from stimulating to impoverished, from social to solitary. Thus, the research design of the brain plasticity studies presents us with a set of three interacting models of educational environments to contemplate in our profession's search for the best use of the limited time we have in our students' lives. The brief introductory discussion below should stimulate your thoughts on the issue.

The Natural Environment. Many educational theorists have proposed over the years that we should move students out of the classroom and into the natural world that students inhabit during their hours outside the school. If that's not possible, they argue that we should at least organize the curriculum around classroom simulations, role playing, field trips, and other activities that more closely parallel the experiences and problem-solving challenges of the natural world.

When done correctly, the much-maligned extracurricular program probably gets as close to real problem solving as anything else we do in school. It uses metaphor, play, and limited adult domination in a nonthreatening, informal setting to explore the dimensions, tactics, and strategies of problem solving. The Duke of Wellington once suggested that the Battle of Waterloo was won on the playing fields of Eton. Play is an important element in a brain's development.

The Laboratory/Classroom Environment. When mature rats were placed in an enriched environment with a group of younger rats, the mature rats played with the toys and dominated the environment. They were stimulated by the environment and developed thicker cortexes. The less-involved younger rats, however, did not experience positive brain development in this potentially stimulating environment (Diamond 1985). These experimental results could find their human representation in classrooms where the teacher dominates the curricular, instructional, and evaluative decisions and activities. It isn't enough for students to be in a stimulating environment—they have to help create it and directly interact with it. They have to have many opportunities to tell *their* stories, not just to listen to the teacher's stories.

What role should teachers play in a classroom that purports to stimulate? John Dewey (1938) commented on the folly of mature adults who work in classrooms with immature students, but don't use their maturity to enhance the students' experience. To use one's maturity, though, doesn't mean to dominate. If we define the most mature person in a social setting as the person in the group who is the most able to adapt to the needs and interests of others, then teachers ought to adapt to their students whenever possible, and not always expect their students to adapt to them.

Such activities as student projects, cooperative learning, and portfolio assessments place students at the center of the educative process, and thus stimulate learning.

The Solitary Environment. It isn't enough to create an environment that merely keeps students busy. Rats placed into a small, solitary cage furnished only with a running wheel stayed active by using the wheel, but experienced no increase in cortical thickness: shades of continual drudgery with workbooks and long division problems. Years of research have found patterns of positive cortical effects only in changing, stimulating, social environments. Rats need to interact with other rats to learn how to solve rat problems. Running a solitary wheel doesn't do the job. The situation is similar with students: a stimulating social setting provides the only appropriate environment for mastering social skills.

Perhaps the most complex educational issue to come out of the human projections of the rat studies is the problem of trying to define a *normal* human environment—beyond the basic properties of being social, changing, and stimulating. Rats flourished best in their normal outdoor habitat. What is the normal habitat of contemporary children and adolescents, the environment that probably has the best potential for developing their brain to its maximum?

It may well be that the limited contemporary classroom and the out-of-school world that many students experience are closer to a natural human habitat than we care to admit. Many families already live in a human version of the enriched social rat cage, with a daily rearrangement of toys sent via TV and consumer technology. It sounds terribly depressing at first thought, and we tend to flog away at our indoor civilization and its electronic artifacts. But I can't think of anything from my childhood that did more to develop eye-hand coordination than the controls on a video game do for my grandchildren. TV and interactive computers have turned our world into a global village, and nobody knows what tomorrow will bring.

We thus need to keep an open mind about our urban electronic culture. We can romanticize the stimulation of a simple life in the great outdoors, but most people live regulated lives that occur primarily indoors—and most of us seem to make the best of it, enriching our lives in imaginative ways that nourish the human spirit.

It's important to remember that the enriched social rat cage did result in significant growth over the impoverished solitary environment. Schools have a responsibility to help students to adapt to the realities of our culture—to enjoy what is good, to resist what is evil. Our profession's major challenge is to create solid enrichment in a social school environment that admittedly has a high potential for impoverishment—to turn an artificial classroom environment into a respectable approximation of a natural human environment.

When pressed to draw practical classroom applications from her years of research with mammalian brains, Marian Diamond smiled and replied that teachers ought to approach their assignment with a commitment to provide their students with *tender loving care.* Tender loving care in the rat studies means that researchers handle rats gently when they work with them. Researchers have discovered that this simple tactile act in itself extends the life span of the animals and, in turn, positively affects their cortical development. Diamond leaves it to educators to discover the human equivalent to her rat care, but she believes that each student should be treated as an individual, with every effort made to bring forth the best in that student.

The discussion above has extrapolated from a rat research environment to a human classroom environment, and such reasoning can introduce problems. At some point we've got to get solid data from humans, so let's turn now to three such research studies. These studies couldn't measure such indicators of brain capability as cortical thickness, as in the rat studies, because they occurred prior to the recent advances in brain-imaging technology that could provide such useful information, but the researchers were able to talk with their research subjects—something the animal researchers couldn't do.

Studies with Hardy and Resilient Human Beings

It's obviously impossible to create a controlled study on the effects of the environment on human brain maturation because such a study would have to rear some of the child subjects in an impoverished environment. Occasionally and tragically, however, a child is reared in such an environment, and so provides useful information on our brain's resilient potential. Genie was one such girl (Rymer 1993).[2]

The Tragic Case of Genie

Authorities discovered 13-year-old Genie in 1970 in the Los Angeles area house where her disturbed father had raised her strapped naked to a potty chair in a back bedroom devoid of sensory stimulation. At night she was placed in the equivalent of a straitjacket in an infant's crib. Her parents rarely spoke to her, and so she had no language skills when she was discovered.

As tragic as her situation was, it created an opportunity for researchers at the University of California at Los Angeles to place her in the caring and stimulating home environment of one of the researchers, and to try to compensate for her years of terrible deprivation with a responsible instructional program. The controversial research studies that emerged out of this process were flawed, but Genie did progress regularly in her ability to walk, eat, talk, and function socially during her five years with the family. Her vocabulary development was quite good, but she was very deficient in sentence structure.

Genie's mother, who had also been victimized by Genie's father, regained custody of Genie at 18, and this legal development unfortunately stopped the research efforts that had attempted to develop her intellectual and language abilities as much as possible. Genie now lives in a home for retarded adults.

We'll never know how much Genie would have developed intellectually and socially with continuous and caring stimulation—and that's too bad for Genie and for those who wonder how much the school and home can do to overcome innate deficiencies and the effects of a traumatic early childhood. But even if the vigorous program of stimulation and instruction had continued, researchers still would never have known what innate potential Genie had. Her father had considered her retarded, and that view helped lead to his inappropriate rearing practices. Considering her terrible childhood, Genie did make astounding and optimistic progress, especially in language development, which linguists had believed was impossible when begun at such a late age.

Genie thus provided us with a rare and tantalizing glimpse into the human equivalent of the plight of the solitary rat in a laboratory cage devoid of any stimulation. As with the rat, she had to leave her solitary, impoverished environment for any hope of adequate cognitive development.

The Hardy Adults

What can our adult brain do when it is seriously challenged by a major life change that it can't control? Hans Selye (1956) and Holmes and Rahe (1967) were pioneering researchers who discovered that chronic stress and major life changes can adversely affect a person's health and consequent ability to cope with life's challenges. Other researchers followed, and one intriguing study examined people who suffered few ill effects in a very stressful situation.

Maddi and Kobasa (1984) studied several hundred middle- and upper-level male managers at AT&T during a very stressful two-year period when the company was being reorganized and their jobs were in jeopardy. About two-thirds of the group suffered stress-related illnesses, but the other third were psychologically hardy, seeming to thrive on the stressful challenges they faced. They experienced less than half the amount of illness experienced by the other high-stress executives.

Maddi and Kobasa discovered that hardy executives who did not suffer the debilitating effects of stress, even though they worked and lived in potentially high-stress environments, demonstrated high levels of *challenge, commitment,* and *control* in their lives. They had learned how to effectively use their brain's problem-solving capabilities:

1. They viewed change as a constant in their life, and welcomed it as a challenge to grow. They approached potentially stressful problems with a clear sense of the importance of their own personal goals, values, and abilities. Realizing that they couldn't do everything, they focused their energies on what they must and could do, and ignored or else sought help for the things they couldn't or shouldn't do. In this, their supervisors respected and supported them.

2. They had a strong commitment to the significant relationships in their life. They identified relationships between major problems and their own clearly defined general life and career

plan, and its established personal, family, and job priorities. They could separate the foreground/background and subjective/objective elements of a problem, and then psychologically separate them. For example, they didn't take personally things that weren't meant to be personal slights, and they didn't take work problems home or bring personal problems to work.

3. They had an internal rather than an external locus of control. Although others may have caused their problem, they assumed responsibility for developing the solution that best met their needs. They didn't consider themselves to be mere victims of circumstance, but rather took personal control of their life, with all its successes and failures.

What we have in this hardy group are people who would make excellent teachers and role models. They would be take-charge teachers with a strong and accepting sense of who they are and what they do, caring teachers who can separate their subjective feelings for their students from the objective demands of their assignment.

What we don't know from this research is whether the ability and personality that allowed these people to function effectively in a very stressful situation came from innate body/brain factors or from a childhood environment that had developed these qualities in them. Therefore, let's look at a study that examined the childhood of high-risk children.

The Resilient Children

In 1955, Emmy Werner and her colleagues began to study about 200 children on the Hawaiian island of Kauai who were considered to be seriously at-risk at birth because of such factors as illness, family poverty, parental discord, and parental mental or medical problems. She has studied them for almost 40 years in an incredible longitudinal study (Werner and Smith 1992). Approximately 700 children were born on the island in 1955, and about 420 of these were born healthy and grew up in supportive environments. The 200 who were at risk because of their health, family, or social environment became the focus of the study.[3]

About two-thirds of these children (129) did not sufficiently overcome their circumstances to create a successful adult life. For example, they developed learning and behavior problems and had delinquency records, mental health problems, and early pregnancies. About one-third (72) of the study group became resilient, however, and adapted successfully to the problems they faced during their growing-up years. The 30 males had a more difficult time adapting to life during their first decade, and the 42 females during their second decade, but today these 72 resilient children have grown up to become successful adults who are living nurturant, responsible, achievement-oriented lives.

Werner and her colleagues identified several personal and environmental factors that they believe played important roles in developing the resilience that the 72 most successful subjects exhibited. She calls these *protective factors* or *buffers*; they protected the young people from their negative environment by providing support, skills, and hope when things looked bleak:

1. The 72 children were of at least average intelligence, and they were healthy, active, sociable children—with a pleasant personality that elicited positive responses from family members and strangers. They were "cuddly" in infancy, interacting easily with others, and this behavior encouraged adults to interact with them in ways that would enhance their intellectual development.

2. They were curious and interacted physically with their environment. As a result of their explorations, they developed interests and hobbies that weren't sex-typed and that they shared with friends.

3. They had both family and nonfamily mentors who provided them with unconditional love. This is an important protective factor, for it provided the resilient children with available positive adult models during a period in which their parents often did not provide such models. One can sense that these mentors encouraged them in their curiosities and hobbies—told them they could become whatever they wanted to be.

4. They were assigned responsibilities in a home environment that was reasonably well-structured. Although some such childhood tasks might be considered exploitative, adults looking back on their childhood often view such assigned tasks as evidence that their parents considered them to be capable and trustworthy. In a study of 500 at-risk students in grades 4 and 5, Kays (1990) found that the alienation from school that many at-risk students were beginning to feel came in part from their noninvolvement in routine classroom tasks that the other students were asked to do. Teachers didn't ask

137

the at-risk students to get the projector, water the plants, or take things to the office. How do children learn to be responsible when they are never asked to be responsible in tasks that others depend on?

5. They developed a positive self-concept and an internal locus of control. Like the Hardy Executives, the Resilient Children were hopeful that when they confronted problems, everything would work out positively.

It's difficult to separate the impact of innate and environmental factors in the Kobasa and Werner studies. Werner noted that the negative effects of problems surrounding pregnancy and birth diminished over time, and the effects of the environment itself became more important. What we don't know, for example, is where the Hardy Executives and Resilient Children would have scored on each of Gardner's forms of intelligence. Were they born with intellectual abilities that tended to put them at the high end of the scales, so that their innate protective factors were strong enough to withstand and solve the problems they faced in their life? We simply don't know.

What we do know is that the middle-aged Hardy Executives were studied during a period of high stress. At that point in their lives they were stimulated by change and challenge, they were committed to themselves and to the significant others in their life, and they had an internal locus of control—a belief that they were responsible for their own life. Educators who possessed these same qualities would be fine role models for students to observe day after day in all sorts of challenging situations.

What we also know is that the Resilient Children were stimulated by other people and functioned effectively around them. They were successful enough in their activities to develop confidence in their interests and abilities, and they also developed an internal locus of control. Such children would profit from interactions with the educators described above. Imagine a classroom full of Resilient Children taught by a Hardy Adult!

The story is not an entirely happy one, however. This discussion focused on the one-third of the executives and at-risk children who were successful and became hardy and resilient. Two-thirds of both groups were not successful. What was the problem? Were their innate protective factors not strong enough, or did their environmental support (e.g., the school) fail them during their developmental years? What a challenge for our profession!

Chapter 1 reported that brain theorists now suggest that we forget the nature versus nurture dichotomy. Rather, we should view the phenomenon as a kind of dynamic interaction of innate and environmental factors. What we have is a classroom full of students who come with genes and nonschool experiences. We're not responsible for the genes, and we usually can't directly do anything about the experiences that students bring to school—but we are responsible for the quality of their school experiences. It's our task to make sure that school experiences enhance the development of a student's brain.

From Brain Theory and Research to School Policy and Practice

As you begin to think through and discuss the information and issues developed in this book—en route to developing school policy and practice attuned to what we're learning about our brain—recall that brain theorists insist that we must now think of our brain as a biological and ecological entity, not as an externally developed and controlled machine, such as a computer.

Thinking about our brain as a computer engenders thoughts of an efficient economical *tool*, something that exists solely to serve others. We do strive to assist and cooperate, but we are also biological entities with our own intrinsic value. We are both a part of and apart from the others who share our environment.

Gerald Edelman suggests that we think of our brain and its processes as being something like the current ecology of a rich jungle environment—in which natural selection and ecological principles operating both over eons of time and within our lifetime have created a magnificent human mind out of a basic human brain. The neural networks we're born with adapt marvelously to a continuously changing and challenging environment. Thus, teachers and parents become *facilitators*, who help to shape a stimulating social environment that helps students to work alone and together to solve the problems they confront.

Ecological principles that enhance the health of the larger environment would then also enhance the development and maintenance

139

of our brain. In *The Closing Circle*, Barry Commoner (1974) proposes four laws of ecology that govern properly operating ecosystems. Since brain theorists view our brain as an ecological system, it might be useful (or at least intriguing) for you and your colleagues to examine Commoner's laws of ecology in the context of considering how to develop an ecologically oriented learning environment for an ecologically evolved brain. The four laws follow, with only enough (sometimes speculative) commentary to get your own curricular and instructional thoughts going:

1. Everything is connected to everything else. Our brain is a dense web of interconnected neurons. Any neuron is only a few neurons away from any other neuron, and all the organisms that inhabit our global village are now also highly interconnected (at least electronically). The naturalist John Muir suggested that when he carefully studied anything in nature, he discovered that it was connected to everything else in the universe. Thus, such things as the language arts, thematic curricula, and multicultural and environmental education programs are central to any curriculum that hopes to help students discover who they are, where they live, and how things are connected.

2. Everything must go somewhere. Everything that occurs within an environment (including a brain environment) leaves a trace. Just as toxic wastes will foul the subsequent life in an environment's ecological chains, so an abusive childhood will be remembered and will affect the child's subsequent life. Just as adding water, sun, and nutrients to an environment enhances the life of organisms in it, so such things as encouragement, help, and praise enhance the learning of students in a school environment.

Although the effects of what we do on a given day in school may not be immediately apparent, they do become part of the rich ecology of the student's life. I don't specifically know when and where I learned about the ecological beauty of the water cycle—except that I learned it in school. I also know that I learned a lot of obscene words and phrases in school.

3. Nature knows best. Complex environments function best through effective processes that have evolved over eons of time. Whether living in an environment or educating students, we must discover and follow the ecological principles that define our brain's capabilities and limitations. We ignore them at our peril: our students misbehave, and our patrons harass us.

The cognitive sciences are now providing much useful information on our brain and its processes, and this book has provided an introduction to that information. But for all practical purposes, that information doesn't exist if we educators don't become aware of it and don't use it in our explorations of how to improve the educative process.

4. There's no such thing as a free lunch. It takes effort to force a system to operate unnaturally (e.g., water flows downhill naturally, but uphill only with great effort). Educational procedures should seek to enhance our brain's strengths and to minimize the negative effects of its weaknesses. For example, we're generally good at such things as cooperating and conceptualizing, at defining moral and ethical issues, at storytelling. We're generally not good at things that require solitary sustained attention and precision.

Suggesting that we might begin to think about curriculum and instruction in the context of Commoner's four laws of ecology (or some other such metaphor) is a simple beginning to the solution of the problem of how best to fit about 100 pounds of student brain into a 1,000-square-foot classroom over a 1,000-hour school year—with at least one adult representative of our culture available to facilitate the operation.

But a simple solution isn't necessarily easy. The challenge of discovering new ways of thinking about what formal education is—and what it can be—is what will make teaching a creative, optimistic, and stimulating profession in the years ahead. It's the continual search for deeper meanings within simple systems that will stimulate imaginative educators to create new forms of enriched social environments within electronic classroom walls.

Current brain theory and research now provide only the broad, tantalizing outlines of what the school of the future might be—but we can anticipate that the rate of new discoveries will escalate. Educators who are willing to study the new cognitive science developments, and then to imaginatively explore and experiment in their search for appropriate educational applications, will have to work out the specifics in the years ahead. If our profession doesn't do it, nothing will happen. Things will remain as they are.

NOTES

Chapter 1

1. Patricia Smith Churchland emphasizes the need for brain researchers and philosophers (and educators) to broaden their perspective of brain/mind in her book *Neurophilosophy: Toward a Unified Science of the Mind/Brain* (Cambridge, Mass.: MIT Press, 1986). It's a fine introduction to neuroscience for philosophers, and to philosophy for neuroscientists. Howard Gardner's *The Mind's New Science: A History of the Cognitive Revolution* (New York: Basic Books, 1985) is an excellent, comprehensive account of the development of the cognitive sciences.

2. Susan Allport's *Explorers of the Black Box: The Search for the Cellular Basis of Memory* (New York: W.W. Norton, 1986) is a fascinating account that focuses on the human side of this extended research, the two principal researchers being Daniel Alkon and Eric Kandel. *Memory's Voice: Deciphering the Brain-Mind Code* (New York: HarperCollins, 1992) is Alkon's autobiographical account of the research.

3. Michael Gazzaniga, one of Roger Sperry's coworkers and a distinguished researcher in his own right, has written an informative, witty, and fascinating account of the 30-year period encompassing the split-brain research in *The Social Brain: Discovering the Networks of the Mind* (New York: Basic Books, 1985). "The Two Brains," the sixth segment of the PBS television series *The Brain* (available on videocassette through PBS Video, 1-800-344-3337), contains an extended discussion with Gazzaniga and others involved in this research.

    William Calvin and George Ojemann's *Conversations with Neil's Brain: The Neural Nature of Thought and Language* (Reading, Mass.: Addison-Wesley, 1994) is a fascinating description of how neurosurgeons now treat serious epileptic cases, and what their work has taught us about language and memory.

4. Michael Posner and Marcus Raichle's *Images of Mind* (New York: Scientific American Library, 1994) is an informative, well-written, and nicely illustrated account of how brain scientists currently use imaging technology. It's written for general readers. Many high school and public libraries have the entire Scientific American Library.

5. The other three books Edelman wrote as he developed his theory are: *The Remembered Present: A Biological Theory of Consciousness* (New York: Basic Books, 1989), *Topobiology: An Introduction to Molecular Embryology* (New York: Basic Books, 1988), and *Neural Darwinism: The Theory of Neuronal Group Selection* (New York: Basic Books, 1987).

See Oliver Sacks, "Making Up The Mind," *The New York Review of Books* (April 8, 1993), pp. 42–49, for an excellent review of *Bright Air, Brilliant Fire*. Steven Levy's "Dr. Edelman's Brain," *The New Yorker* (May 2, 1994), pp. 62–73, is an informative profile of Edelman and his theory. Michael Gazzaniga's *Nature's Mind: The Biological Roots of Thinking, Emotions, Sexuality, Language, and Intelligence* (New York: Basic Books, 1992) and Robert Ornstein's *The Evolution of Consciousness: The Origins of the Way We Think* (New York: Prentic Hall Press, 1991) are informative nontechnical discussions of the general thrust of the current theoretical work.

6. William Calvin, "The Emergence of Intelligence," *Scientific American* (October 1994): 101-107, describes six processes that define Darwinian evolution and suggests how they relate to genetics, immunology, and brain development: (1) The biological process operates on patterns, such as DNA. (2) These patterns are copied. (3) Patterns must occasionally vary, such as through mutations or copying errors. (4) Variant patterns must compete to occupy some limited space. (5) The environment influences the relative reproductive success of the variants, and this is called *natural selection*. (6) The makeup of the next generation of patterns depends on which variants survive to be copied.

Chapter 2

1. Anne D. Novitt-Moreno's *How Your Brain Works* (Emeryville, Calif.: Ziff-Davis) is a beautifully illustrated, clearly written manual of our brain and its processes, and therefore is an excellent companion to this book.

2. Richard Restak's *Receptors* (New York: Bantam, 1994) is a fascinating nontechnical explanation of the important role that receptors play in the operation of our body/brain.

3. Richard Restak's *The Modular Brain* (New York: Scribners, 1994) is an excellent nontechnical explanation of the concept of a modular brain, and of the evidence to support the concept.

4. This organization holds for almost all right-handed people and about two-thirds of left-handed people. The others have reversed hemisphere specializations or some other organization.

Chapter 3

1. Smell provides an interesting example of how species tune their sensory systems to their environment. Most four-legged animals have a much stronger sense of smell than we have, and we have a more powerful visual system than they have. One possible reason is that odor molecules are heavy, and so tend to settle near the ground (where four-legged animals' noses often are, sniffing about for food). To experience this height variation in odor, breathe deeply on a calm, warm summer day, then lie down on the grass and breathe again. Note the difference as the rich mix of odors

suddenly rushes into your brain. When early humans stood up on two legs and so moved their head several feet from the ground, where the view was less obstructed, smell became less useful and vision became more useful. Over evolutionary time, the relative strength of the two systems reversed.

2. Recent discoveries indicate that dyslexia can result from a lack of coordination in the fast (magnocellular) and slow (parvocellular) pathways in the visual and auditory systems. Discoveries about the visual system appear in M. Livingstone et al., "Physiological and Anatomical Evidence for a Magnocellular Defect in Developmental Dyslexia, "*Proceedings of the National Academy of Science* 88 (September 1991): 7943-7947. Discoveries about the auditory system appear in A. Galaburda, M. Menard, and G. Rosen, "Evidence for Aberrant Auditory Anatomy in Developmental Dyslexia," *Proceedings of the National Academy of Science* 91 (August 1994): 8010-8013.

3. Diane Ackerman, a poet, has written a delightful nontechnical explanation and exploration of our sensory system and its cultural ramifications, *A Natural History of the Senses* (New York: Random House, 1990). It contains many marvelous ideas that imaginative teachers could incorporate into an instructional unit on the sensory system. In early 1995, PBS aired *Mystery of the Senses,* a NOVA miniseries based on this book. The June 1993 issue of *Discover* magazine is an interesting and informative special issue that focuses on our sensory system.

4. David Hubel, who won a Nobel Prize for his work on the visual system, has written an excellent explanation of the biology of the system for general readers, *Eye, Brain, and Vision* (New York: W.H. Freeman, 1988).

5. An interesting way to note time and distance differences in the movement of touch information is to tap your nose with your index finger and note whether you felt the tap principally in your nose or your finger. Then use *the same finger* to tap an ankle, and again note whether you principally felt the tap in your finger or your ankle. The chances are good that you felt the tap in your nose rather than your finger because your nose is closer to your brain than your finger, but in your finger rather than your ankle because your finger is closer to your brain than your ankle.

6. Ashley Montagu's *Touching: The Human Significance of the Skin* (New York: Harper and Row, 1978) is a fascinating nontechnical resource on our skin and its cultural significance.

7. Patrick Suskind's *Perfume* (New York: Knopf, 1987) is a fascinating novel about a person with an extraordinary sense of smell, but the book also provides much interesting information on our sense of smell.

8. Although the taking in of food and drink and the consequent beginning of the digestive process tends to be social, celebratory, and romantic, the inevitable conclusion of the process tends to be solitary and neither celebratory nor romantic. Our language is rich with terms that describe and laud eating and drinking, but terms for defecation and urination are spoken of

in euphemisms or in terms that are part of the darker realm of our language—and the processes themselves are part of our shame culture. It's interesting to muse beyond food and drink to the social, celebratory, and romantic taking in of culture and information (such as at concerts, theaters, churches, and schools) and to the shame that we associate with the things we discard because the system couldn't assimilate them—the plays that didn't get produced, the students who failed.

9. You've probably at some time been walking along and carrying on a conversation with a friend when you were confronted by a physical obstruction. You and your friend both probably stopped talking while you walked around the obstruction. In this common experience, we have an example of the shift from unconscious behavior (walking along without obstructions) to conscious behavior (walking around an obstruction) interfering with another conscious behavior (the conversation).

Chapter 4

1. Richard Cytowic's *The Man Who Tasted Shapes* (New York: G.P. Putnam, 1993) is a fascinating nontechnical account of people who have synesthesia, a rare condition that gives them cross-modal sensory awareness (they see sounds, hear colors, etc.). Such people provide a conscious window into our emotional system, a window that Cytowic marvelously explores.

    Antonio Damasio's *Descarte's Error: Emotion, Reason, and the Human Brain* (New York: Grosset/Putnam, 1994) describes how scientists used modern computers to reconstruct the terrible brain injury that Phineas Gage suffered a century ago when a pipe propelled through his brain, but didn't kill him. Damasio's research led to major discoveries about our emotions.

2. Our sensory system is tuned to contrast. Individual sensory receptors compare the information received within their narrow field in time and space with surrounding receptors. If the information is similar (e.g., white next to white, or cold next to cold), the information is forwarded into the brain with less strength than if the two sets of information differ (e.g., white next to black, cold next to warm). And so we tend to notice lines (white/black) more than solid areas (white/white or black/black), and we note the heat differential when we step from a warm room into the cold outside. Two minutes later, however, when it's cold next to cold, we are less aware of the cold.

3. Our brainstem passively receives incoming sensory information and begins the process of active attention. Two brainstem structures appear to control arousal and our ability to ignore irrelevant stimuli: (1) the reticular formation, a sort of chemical net that fluctuates in 90-minute cycles across the 24 hours to allow different amounts of sensory/motor information to enter and leave our brain, and (2) the locus coeruleus, a small but important structure that synthesizes and distributes norepinephrine throughout our brain to activate networks. Its some 20,000 neurons are synaptically connected to five billion other neurons. The raphe nucleus, a small structure that synthesizes

serotonin and distributes it throughout our brain, also helps to regulate the system.

4. Norepinephrine and dopamine (forming a class of neurotransmitters) appear to be the principal neurotransmitter systems that process attention. Schizophrenia appears to involve excessive catecholamine activity, and some forms of hyperactivity may involve an insufficient number of catecholamines. Attention seems to function best with an optimum middle level of catecholamines.

5. We awake in the morning after an extended period of fasting, and so it was important for early humans to be alert in the morning in their search of food. Assuming that they located food, their alertness could drop off in the afternoon, but they needed to remain wary because of predators that were still searching for food. Our modern brain continues to follow the same daily chemical rhythms. J. Alan Hobson's *The Chemistry of Conscious States: How the Brain Changes Its Mind* (Boston: Little Brown, 1994) is an excellent nontechnical explanation of our attentional system.

6. A good source on the psychobiology of ADHD for general readers is: G.W. Hynde, et al., "Neurobiological Basis of Attention Deficit Hyperactivity Disorder" *School Psychology Review* 20, 2 (1991): 174-186. A recent nontechnical report, "Life in Overdrive," is the cover story in the July 18, 1994, issue of *Time*, pp. 42-50.

7. This attempt to reverse background and foreground has also occurred in several highly publicized court cases in which the defense depicted the accused as victims, and the victims as perpetrators; in some cases foreground and background were reversed, in others they weren't. In the context of brain functions, what's most interesting about these cases is not the guilt or innocence of the accused, but the difficulty of determining what's important and unimportant, true and false, right and wrong, when experts who are highly effective in influencing opinion are brought in to shape political and legal battles.

Chapter 5

1. Norepinephrine (or adrenaline, when it's a hormone) is associated with both alertness and the stress response. Chapter 2 described the actions of the endorphins, a class of peptides that reduce awareness of pain in dangerous situations in which the pain might immobilize a person who might need to escape. The release of endorphins in an emotionally painful or hurtful situation, as described in the text, might thus interfere with the development of a memory. Appendix A also contains information on the neurotransmitters.

2. Elizabeth Loftus is a major memory researcher who questions the validity of repressed memories. In *The Myth of Repressed Memories* (New York: St. Martin's Press, 1994), she cites research studies in which subjects were led

to fabricate entire memories of traumatic events from their childhood that hadn't occurred.

3.   The norepinephrine and serotonin neurotransmitter systems that play an important role in maintaining attention when we're awake reduce their activity during non-REM sleep and shut down during REM sleep, when we dream. The acetylcholine neurotransmitter system, which is active when we're awake, begins to dominate brain activity during sleep, especially during dream periods. Acetylcholine plays an important role in the operation of the hippocampus, which codes long-term memories. Hobson's *The Chemistry of Conscious States* (Boston: Little, Brown, 1994) provides a clear explanation of the process.

Chapter 6

1.   Gardner has expanded his ideas in three subsequent books (all published by Basic Books), *The Unschooled Mind: How Children Think and How Schools Should Teach* (1991), *Multiple Intelligences: The Theory in Practice* (1993), and *Creating Minds* (1993), an analysis of recognized geniuses who represent each of Gardner's multiple intelligences. Thomas Armstrong's *Multiple Intelligences in the Classroom* (Alexandria, Va.: ASCD, 1994) suggests practical classroom activities for educators who are interested in exploring Gardner's theory.

2.   This arrangement differs somewhat from that of Gardner, who arranged the seven forms of intelligence into (1) *object-related* forms of intelligence (spatial, logical-mathematical, bodily-kinesthetic) that depend on controls that emerge out of the structure and function of the objects we confront, (2) *object-free* forms of intelligence (language, music) that don't emerge out of the physical world, but rather reflect the structure and function of body systems, and (3) *personal* forms of intelligence that reflect the possibilities and constraints of self, others, and culture.

3.   It isn't clear what purpose music serves, or what natural selection advantages it provides to the human race. Birdsong plays an important role in the mating rituals of birds, and much of our music also focuses on mating and bonding behaviors.

4.   The November 1994 issue of *Discover* magazine is devoted to a thoughtful and thought-provoking analysis of the science of race. It's important to realize that race accounts for only 6 percent of the biological differences in humans, and that it's possible to group humans on the basis of other genetic differences that may show normative differences in intelligence. For example, fingerprint patterns are genetic, and so we could group humans into those who have many loops (e.g., Europeans, black Africans), many arches (e.g., Jews, Indonesians), and many whorls (e.g., Aboriginal Australians)—and then possibly identify normative intellectual differences among those

three groups. But so what? What logical relationship exists between finger-print patterns and intelligence—or between skin color and intelligence?

5. This summary also draws heavily on material from two articles that I wrote with Chris Hasegawa (now of Sacramento State University, Calif.): "How to Explain Drugs to Your Students," *Middle School Journal* (January 1989), and "Drug Education and the Science Teacher," *The Oregon Science Teacher* (January 1988).

Chapter 7

1. Both Piaget and Epstein did their research during periods in which it was very difficult to measure the subtle intellectual and brain differences they were studying, and some critics felt they went beyond their data. Epstein refuted his critics in a 1986 article, "Stages in Human Growth Development," published in a very respected scientific journal, *Developmental Brain Research* 30: 114–119. Although they were essentially biologists and not K–12 educa-tors, Piaget and Epstein made major contributions to education by getting educators to think about their students in biological terms.

2. Russ Rymer's *Genie: An Abused Child's Flight from Silence* (New York: Har-perCollins, 1993) and the PBS *NOVA* episode "The Secrets of the Wild Child" (with extended videotape of Genie) provide haunting, fascinating, and thought-provoking perspectives of Genie and her tragic situation. (Video-cassette available through WGBH; call 1-800-255-9424.)

3. Emmy Werner and Ruth Smith's most recent report on their study, *Overcom-ing the Odds: High Risk Children from Birth to Adulthood* (Ithaca, N.Y.: Cornell University Press, 1992) is fascinating and informative—a marvelous source for educators who work with at-risk students, but also for those who want a positive boost on a day when everything looks bleak.

BIBLIOGRAPHY

Ackerman, D. (1990). *A Natural History of the Senses*. New York: Random House

Ackerman, D. (1994). *A Natural History of Love*. New York: Random House.

Ackerman, S. (1992). *Discovering the Brain*. Washington D.C.: National Academy Press.

Aggleton, J.P., ed. (1992). *The Amygdala: Neurological Aspects of Emotion, Memory, and Mental Dysfunction*. New York: Wiley-Liss.

Alkon, D.L. (1992). *Memory's Voice: Deciphering the Brain-Mind Code*. New York: HarperCollins.

Allman, W.F. (1989). *Apprentices of Wonder: Inside the Neural Network Revolution*. New York: Bantam.

Allport, A. (1989). "Visual Attention." In *Foundations of Cognitive Science*, edited by M.I. Posner. Cambridge, Mass.: MIT Press.

Allport, S. (1986). *Explorers of the Black Box: The Search for the Cellular Basis of Memory*. New York: W.W. Norton.

Armstrong, T. (1994). *Multiple Intelligences in the Classroom*. Alexandria, Va.: ASCD.

Atkins, P.W. (1987). *Molecules*. New York: W.H. Freeman.

Baddeley, A.D. (1993). *Your Memory: A User's Guide*. Garden City Park, N.Y.: Avery.

Barondes, S.H. (1993). *Molecules and Mental Illness*. New York: Scientific American Library.

Bergland, R. (1985). *The Fabric of Mind*. New York: Penguin.

Binkley, S. (1990). *The Clockwork Sparrow: Time, Clocks, and Calendars in Biological Organisms*. Englewood Cliffs, N.J.: Prentice Hall.

Blakeslee, S. (June 1, 1993). "Scanner Pinpoints Sites of Thought as People See or Speak." *New York Times*, Section C, pp. 1, 3.

Bloom, F.E. , A. Lazerson, and L. Hofstadter. (1985). *Brain, Mind, and Behavior*. New York: W.H. Freeman.

Bolles, E.B. (1988). *Remembering and Forgetting: An Inquiry into the Nature of Memory*. New York: Walker.

Bolles, E.B. (1991). *A Second Way of Knowing: The Riddle of Human Perception*. New York: Prentice Hall.

Bootzin, R.R., J.F. Kihlstrom, and D.L. Schacter. (1990). *Sleep and Cognition*. Washington D.C.: American Psychological Association.

The Brain. (1984). Produced by WNET/New York, Antenne 2 TV/France, and NHK/Japan for distribution by PBS. (8 videocassettes).

Caine, R., and G. Caine. (1994). *Making Connections: Teaching and the Human Brain*. Alexandria, Va.: ASCD.

Calvin, W. (1990). *The Cerebral Symphony: Seashore Reflections on the Structure of Consciousness*. New York: Bantam.

Calvin, W. (1991). *The Ascent of Mind: Ice Age Climates and the Evolution of Intelligence.* New York: Bantam.

Calvin, W. (October 1994). "The Emergence of Intelligence." *Scientific American Magazine* 271, 4: 101–107.

Calvin, W.A., and G.A. Ojemann. (1994). *Conversations with Neil's Brain: The Neural Nature of Thought and Language.* Reading, Mass.: Addison-Wesley.

Campbell, J. (1986). *Winston Churchill's Afternoon Nap: A Wide-Awake Inquiry into the Human Nature of Time.* New York: Simon and Schuster.

Campbell, J. (1989). *The Improbable Machine: What the Upheavals in Artificial Intelligence Research Reveal About How the Mind Really Works.* New York: Simon and Schuster.

Changeux, J. (1985). *Neuronal Man: The Biology of Mind.* New York: Pantheon.

Cho, J.Y. (1990). *Attention: Cognitive Science Discoveries and Educational Practice.* Doctoral diss., University of Oregon.

Churchland, P.S. (1986). *Neurophilosophy: Toward a Unified Science of the Mind-Brain.* Cambridge, Mass.: MIT Press.

Churchland, P., and T.J. Sejnowski. (1992). *The Computational Brain.* Cambridge, Mass.: MIT Press.

Clark, M., et al. (January 12, 1987). "A User's Guide to Hormones." *Newsweek,* pp. 50–59.

Commoner, B. (1974). *The Closing Circle: Nature, Man, and Technology.* New York: Bantam.

Corballis, M.C. (1991). *The Lopsided Ape: Evolution of the Generative Mind.* New York: Oxford University Press.

Crapo, L. (1985). *Hormones, the Messengers of Life.* New York: W.H. Freeman.

Crick, F. (1994). *The Astonishing Hypothesis: The Scientific Search for the Soul.* New York: Scribner; New York: Maxwell Macmillan International.

Crick, F., and G. Mitchison. (1983). "The Function of Dream Sleep." *Nature* 304: 111–114.

Cytowic, R.E. (1993). *The Man Who Tasted Shapes.* New York: G.P. Putnam.

Damasio, A. (1994). *Descarte's Error: Emotion, Reason, and the Human Brain.* New York: Grosset/Putnam.

Dewey, J. (1938). *Experience and Education.* New York: Macmillan.

Diamond, M., A. Scheibel, G. Murphy, and T. Harvey. (1985a). "On the Brain of a Scientist: Albert Einstein." *Experimental Neurology* 88: 198–204.

Diamond, M.C. (1985b). "Cortical Plasticity Induced by Experience and Sex Hormones." Paper presented at the California Neuropsychological Services Conference, San Raphael, Calif.

Diamond, M.C. (1988). *Enriching Heredity: The Impact of the Environment on the Anatomy of the Brain.* New York: Free Press.

Dienstfrey, H. (1991). *Where the Mind Meets the Body.* New York: HarperCollins.

Discover magazine. (June 1993). A special issue devoted to the sensory system.

Discover magazine. (November 1994). A special issue devoted to the science of race.

Donald, M. (1991). *Origins of the Modern Mind: Three Stages in the Evolution of Culture and Cognition.* Cambridge, Mass.: Harvard University Press.

Dozier Jr., R.J. (1992). *Codes of Evolution: The Synaptic Language Revealing the Secrets of Matter, Life, and Thought.* New York: Crown.

Edelman, G.M. (1987). *Neural Darwinism: The Theory of Neuronal Group Selection.* New York: Basic Books.

Edelman, G.M. (1988). *Topobiology: An Introduction to Molecular Embryology.* New York: Basic Books.

Edelman, G.M. (1989). *The Remembered Present: A Biological Theory of Consciousness.* New York: Basic Books.

Edelman, G.M. (1992). *Bright Air, Brilliant Fire: On the Matter of the Mind.* New York: Basic Books.

Epstein, H. (1978). "Growth Spurts During Brain Development: Implications for Educational Policy and Practice." In *Education and the Brain: 77th National Society for the Study of Education Yearbook,* edited by J. Chall and A. Mirsky. Chicago: University of Chicago Press.

Epstein, H. (1986). "Stages in Human Brain Development." *Developmental Brain Research* 30: 114–19.

Flavell, J.H. (1963). *The Developmental Psychology of Jean Piaget.* Princeton N.J.: Van Nostrand.

Fluckiger, E., E. Muller, and M. Thorner. (1987). *Transmitter Molecules in the Brain.* New York: Springer-Verlag.

Franklin, J. (1987). *Molecules of the Mind: The Brave New Science of Molecular Psychology.* New York: Atheneum.

Friedman, S.L., K.A. Klivington, and R.W. Peterson, eds. (1986). *The Brain, Cognition, and Education.* Orlando, Fla.: Academic Press.

Galaburda, A.M., ed. (1993). *Dyslexia and Development: Neurobiological Aspects of Extra-Ordinary Brains.* Cambridge, Mass.: Harvard University Press.

Galaburda, A., M. Menard, and G. Rosen. (August 1994). "Evidence for Aberrant Auditory Anatomy in Developmental Dyslexia." *Proceedings of the National Academy of Science* 91: 8010–8013.

Gardner, H. (1983). *Frames of Mind: The Theory of Multiple Intelligences.* New York: Basic Books.

Gardner, H. (1985). *The Mind's New Science: A History of the Cognitive Revolution.* New York: Basic Books.

Gardner, H. (1991). *The Unschooled Mind: How Children Think and How Schools Should Teach.* New York: Basic Books.

Gardner, H. (1993). *Creating Minds.* New York: Basic Books.

Gardner, H. (1993). *Multiple Intelligences: The Theory in Practice.* New York: Basic Books.

Garmezy, N., and M. Rutter, eds. (1988). *Stress, Coping, and Development in Children.* Baltimore: Johns Hopkins University Press.

Gazzaniga, M. (1985). *The Social Brain: Discovering the Networks of the Mind.* New York: Basic Books.

Gazzaniga, M. (1988a). *Mind Matters: How Mind and Brain Interact to Create Our Conscious Lives.* Boston: Houghton Mifflin, in association with MIT Press.

Gazzaniga, M., ed. (1988b). *Perspectives in Memory Research.* Cambridge, Mass.: MIT Press.

Gazzaniga, M. (1992). *Nature's Mind: The Biological Roots of Thinking, Emotions, Sexuality, Language, and Intelligence.* New York: Basic Books.

Goode, E. (June 21, 1991). "Where Emotions Come From." *U.S. News and World Report,* pp. 54-62.

Goodsell, D.S. (1993). *The Machinery of Life.* New York: Springer-Verlag.

Gray, P. (February 15, 1993). "The Chemistry of Love." *Time* 141, 7: 46–51.

Gregory, R.L., ed. (1987). *The Oxford Companion to the Mind.* New York: Oxford University Press.

Harth, E. (1993). *The Creative Loop: How the Brain Makes a Mind.* Reading, Mass.: Addison-Wesley.

Hasegawa, C., and R. Sylwester. (Jauary 1988). "Drug Education and the Science Teacher." *The Oregon Science Teacher.*

Herrnstein, R.J., and C. Murray. (1994). *The Bell Curve: Intelligence and Class Structure in American Life.* New York: Free Press.

Hobson, J. (1989). *Sleep.* New York: Scientific American Library. Distributed by W.H. Freeman.

Hobson, J.A. (1994). *The Chemistry of Conscious States: How the Brain Changes Its Mind.* Boston: Little, Brown.

Holmes, T., and R. Rahe. (1967). "The Social Readjustment Rating Scale." *Journal of Psychometric Research* 11: 213–218.

Hubel, D.H. (1988). *Eye, Brain, and Vision.* New York: W.H. Freeman.

Humphrey, N. (1992). *A History of the Mind: Evolution and the Birth of Consciousness.* New York: Simon and Schuster.

Hynde, G. W., et al. (1991). "Neurobiological Basis of Attention Deficit Hyperactivity Disorder." *School Psychology Review* 20, 2: 174–186.

Isaacson, R.L. (1982). *The Limbic System.* 2nd ed. New York: Plenum Press.

Jackendoff, R. (1994). *Patterns in the Mind: Language and Human Behavior.* New York: Basic Books.

Johnson, G. (1991). *In the Palaces of Memory: How We Build the Worlds Inside Our Heads.* New York: Knopf. Distributed by Random House.

Joseph, R. (1992). *The Right Brain and the Unconscious: Discovering the Stranger Within.* New York: Plenum.

Joseph, R. (1993). *The Naked Neuron: Evolution and the Languages of the Body and Brain.* New York: Plenum.

Julien, R.M. (1985). *A Primer of Drug Action.* 4th ed. New York: W.H. Freeman.

Kandel, M., and E. Kandel. (May 1994). "Flights of Memory." *Discover* 15, 6: 32–38.

Kays, D. (1990). *A Comparison of the Attendance Rates and Patterns of Fourth and Fifth Grade At-Risk and Not At-Risk Students in 27 Elementary Schools.* Doctoral diss., University of Oregon, Eugene.

Kimble, D.P. (1988). *Biological Psychology.* New York: Holt Rinehart Winston.

Kimmelberg, H., and M. Norenberg. (April 1989). "Astrocytes." *Scientific American*, pp. 66–76.

Klivington, K. (1986). "Building Bridges Among Neuroscience, Cognitive Psychology, and Education." In *The Brain, Cognition, and Learning*, edited by S. Friedman, K. Klivington, and R. Peterson. New York: Academic Press.

Klivington, K., ed. (1989). *The Science of Mind*. Cambridge, Mass.: MIT Press.

Kobasa, S. (January 1979). "Stressful Life Events, Personality, and Health: An Inquiry into Hardiness." *Journal of Personality and Social Psychology* 37: 1–11.

Kobasa, S. (1990). "Stress-Resistant Personality." In *The Healing Brain: A Scientific Reader*, edited by R. Ornstein and C. Swencionis. New York: Guilford Press.

Kosslyn, S.M., and O. Koenig. (1992). *Wet Mind: The New Cognitive Neuroscience*. New York: Free Press.

Lashley, K. (1950). "In Search of the Engram." *Society for Experimental Biology Symposium #4: Mechanisms in Animal Behavior*. New York: Cambridge University Press.

LeDoux, J.E. (June 1994). "Emotion, Memory, and Brain." *Scientific American* 270, 6: 50–57.

LeDoux, J.E., and W. Hirst, eds. (1986). *Mind and Brain: Dialogues in Cognitive Neuroscience*. New York: Cambridge University Press.

LeVay, S. (1993). *The Sexual Brain*. Cambridge, Mass.: MIT Press.

LeVay, S., and D. Hamer. (May 1994). "Debate: Evidence for a Biological Influence in Male Homosexuality." *Scientific American* 270, 5: 43–58.

Levinthal, C.F. (1988). *Messengers of Paradise: Opiates and the Brain*. New York: Anchor Press/Doubleday.

Levy, S. (May 2, 1994). "Dr. Edelman's Brain." *The New Yorker*, pp. 62–74.

Livingstone, M., et al. (September 1991). "Physiological and Anatomical Evidence for a Magnocellular Defect in Developmental Dyslexia." *Proceedings of the National Academy of Science* 88: 7943–7947.

Loftus, E.F. (1994). *The Myth of Repressed Memory: False Memories and Allegations of Sexual Abuse*. New York: St. Martin's Press.

Luria, A.R. (1968). *The Mind of a Mnemonist*. New York: Basic Books.

MacLean, P. (1978). "A Mind of Three Minds: Educating the Triune Brain." In *Education and the Brain, 77th National Society for the Study of Education Yearbook*, edited by J. Chall, and A. Mirsky. Chicago: University of Chicago Press.

Maddi, S.R., and S.C. Kobasa. (1984). *The Hardy Executive: Health under Stress*. Homewood, Ill.: Dow Jones-Irwin.

Madden, J., ed. (1991). *Neurobiology of Learning, Emotion, and Affect*. New York: Raven Press.

Maguire, J. (1990). *Care and Feeding of the Brain: A Guide to Your Gray Matter*. New York: Doubleday.

Masters, R.D., and M.T. McGuire, eds. (1994). *The Neurotransmitter Revolution: Serotonin, Behavior, and the Law*. Carbondale, Ill.: Southern Illinois University Press.

Maturana, H.R., and F.J. Varela. (1987). *The Tree of Knowledge: The Biological Roots of Human Understanding.* Boston: New Science Library. Distributed by Random House.

Minsky, M. (1986). *The Society of Mind.* New York: Simon and Schuster.

Moir, A., and D. Jessel. (1991). *Brain Sex: The Real Differences Between Men and Women.* New York: Carol Publishing Group.

Monat, A., and R.S. Lazarus, eds. (1991). *Stress and Coping.* New York: Columbia University Press.

Montagu, A. (1978). *Touching: The Human Significance of the Skin.* 2nd ed. New York: Harper and Row.

Moyers, B. (1993). *Healing and the Mind,* edited by B.S. Flowers. New York: Doubleday.

Mystery of the Senses: A NOVA Miniseries. (1994). Developed by WETA Washington, D.C. Series produced by Peter Jones. (Video series available thru WGBH; call 1-800-255-9424.)

Neisser, U. (1982). *Memory Observed: Remembering in Natural Contexts.* San Francisco: W.H. Freeman.

Novitt-Moreno, Anne D. (1995). *How Your Brain Works,* illustrated by Erika Luikart. Emeryville, Calif.: Ziff-Davis.

Ornstein, R. (1991). *The Evolution of Consciousness: The Origins of the Way We Think.* New York: Prentice Hall Press.

Ornstein, R. (1993). *The Roots of the Self: Unraveling the Mystery of Who We Are.* San Francisco: HarperCollins.

Ornstein, R.E., and P. Ehrlich. (1989). *New World, New Mind: Moving Toward Conscious Evolution.* New York: Doubleday.

Ornstein, R., and D. Sobel. (1987). *The Healing Brain: Breakthrough Discoveries About How the Brain Keeps Us Healthy.* New York: Simon and Schuster.

Ornstein, R., and C. Swencionis, eds. (1990). *The Healing Brain: A Scientific Reader.* New York: Guilford Press.

Pool, R.E. (1994). *Eve's Rib: The Biological Roots of Sex Differences.* New York: Crown.

Posner, M.I., ed. (1989). *Foundations of Cognitive Science.* Cambridge, Mass.: MIT Press.

Posner, M.I., and M.E. Raichle (1994). *Images of Mind.* New York: Scientific American Library.

Purves, D. (1988). *Body and Brain: A Trophic Theory of Neural Conections.* Cambridge, Mass.: Harvard University Press.

Raichle, M. (1993). Lecture at the American Academy of Neurology, New York City.

Reiser, M.F. (1984). *Mind, Brain, Body: Toward a Convergence of Psychoanalysis and Neurobiology.* New York: Basic Books.

Reiser, M.F. (1990). *Memory in Mind and Brain: What Dream Imagery Reveals.* New York: Basic Books.

Restak, R. (1994). *The Modular Brain.* New York: Scribner.

Restak, R. (1994). *Receptors.* New York: Bantam.

Rose, K.J. (1988). *The Body in Time.* New York: Wiley.

Rose. S. (1993). *The Making of Memory: From Molecules to Mind.* New York: Anchor Books/Doubleday.

Rosenfield, I. (1988). *The Invention of Memory: A New View of the Brain.* New York: Basic Books.

Rosenfield, I. (1992). *The Strange, Familiar, and Forgotten: An Anatomy of Consciousness.* New York: Knopf.

Rosenzweig, M., R. Bennett, and M. Diamond. (1972). "Brain Changes in Response to Experience." *Scientific American* 226: 22–29.

Rymer, R. (1993). *Genie: An Abused Child's Flight from Silence.* New York: Harper-Collins.

Saarni, C., and P.L. Harris, eds. (1989). *Children's Understanding of Emotion.* New York: Cambridge University Press.

Sacks, O. (April 8, 1993). "Making Up The Mind, A Review-Essay of Gerald Edelman's *Bright Air, Brilliant Fire.*" *The New York Review of Books,* pp. 42–49.

Schank, R.C. (1990). *Tell Me A Story: A New Look at Real and Artificial Memory.* New York: Scribner.

Schank, R.C. (1991). *The Connoisseur's Guide to the Mind: How We Think, How We Learn, and What It Means to Be Intelligent.* New York: Summit Books.

Scientific American. (September 1992). "Mind and Brain." A special issue devoted to brain theory and research.

Scientific American. (September 1993). "Life, Death, and the Immune System." A special issue devoted to recent developments in immunology.

"The Secrets of the Wild Child." Episode of *NOVA* series on public television. (Videocassette available thru WGBH; call 1-800-255-9424.)

Selye, H. (1956, revised 1976). *The Stress of Life.* New York: McGraw-Hill.

Simonov, P.V. (1986). *The Emotional Brain: Physiology, Neuroanatomy, Psychology, Emotion,* translated from the Russian by M.J. Hall. New York: Plenum.

Smith, J. (1989). *Senses and Sensibilities.* New York: Wiley.

Snyder, S.H. (1986). *Drugs and the Brain.* New York: Scientific American Books. Distributed by W.H. Freeman.

Society for Neuroscience. (1990). *Brain Facts: A Primer on the Brain and Nervous System.* Washington D.C.: Society for Neuroscience.

Springer, S.P., and G. Deutsch. (1989). *Left Brain, Right Brain.* 3rd. ed. New York: W.H. Freeman.

Stein, K. (June 1994). "Mind Reading Among the Macaques: How the Brain Interprets the Intentions of Others." *Omni* 16, 9: 10.

Sternberg, R. (1988). *The Triarchic Mind: A New Theory of Human Intelligence.* New York: Viking.

Suskind, P. (1987). *Perfume: The Story of a Murderer.* New York: Knopf.

Sylwester, R. (April 1985). "Research on Memory: Major Discoveries, Major Educational Challenges." *Educational Leadership* 42, 7: 69–75.

Sylwester, R. (Summer 1986). "Learning About Learning: The Neurosciences and the Education Profession." *Educational Horizons* 64, 4: 162–167.

Sylwester, R. (September 1986). "Synthesis of Research on Brain Plasticity: The Classroom Environment and Curriculum Enrichment." *Educational Leadership* 44, 1: 90–93.

Sylwester, R. (April 1990). "Separating Foreground from Background: Brain Mechanisms and School Practices." *Elementary School Guidance and Counseling* 24, 4: 289–297.

Sylwester, R. (October 1990). "Expanding the Range, Dividing the Task: Educating the Human Brain in an Electronic Society." *Educational Leadership* 48, 2: 71–78.

Sylwester, R. (1991). "How Our Brain Is Organized Along Three Planes to Process Complexity, Context, and Continuity." In *Developing Minds: A Resource Book for Teaching Thinking,* edited by A. Costa. Alexandria, Va.: ASCD.

Sylwester, R., and C. Hasegawa (January 1989). "How to Explain Drugs to Your Students." *Middle School Journal* : 8–11.

Sylwester, R., and J. Cho. (December 1992). "What Brain Research Says About Paying Attention." *Educational Leadership* 40, 5: 71–75.

Thayer, R.E. (1989). *The Biopsychology of Mood and Arousal.* New York: Oxford University Press.

Vincent, J.D. (1990). *The Biology of Emotions,* translated by J. Hughes. Cambridge, Mass.: Basil Blackwell.

Werner, E., and R. Smith. (1992). *Overcoming the Odds: High Risk Children from Birth to Adulthood.* Ithaca N.Y.: Cornell University Press.

Wills, C. (1993). *The Runaway Brain: The Evolution of Human Uniqueness.* New York: Basic Books.

Winfree, A.T. (1987). *The Timing of Biological Clocks.* New York: W.H. Freeman.

Wolf, F.A. (1994). *The Dreaming Universe: A Mind-Expanding Journey into the Realm Where Psyche and Physics Meet.* New York: Simon and Schuster.

APPENDIX A

Neurotransmitter Systems
and Related Drug Actions

Amino Acids

The four amino acid neurotransmitters have the simplest molecular structure of the various neurotransmitters. These fast-acting neurotransmitters are widely distributed throughout our brain and spinal cord, with concentrations 1,000 times greater than the monoamines.

Glutamate (or glutamic acid) and *asparte* always carry an excitatory message. Glutamate is the principal excitatory neurotransmitter in the cerebral cortex and cerebellum, and it appears to play an important role in vision, learning, and memory.

GABA and *glycine* always carry an inhibitory message. GABA (gamma-aminobutyric acid) is the principal inhibitory neurotransmitter in the cortex (with as many as one-third of all synapses being GABA synapses), and it's also found in the limbic system. GABA circuits reduce anxiety and relax muscles. Glycine is a major neurotransmitter in the brainstem and spinal cord.

Monoamines

The six monoamine neurotransmitters are chemically modified amino acids that act more slowly than the amino acids. Their circuitry diverges from a single brainstem or limbic system source and then spreads widely throughout the brain, where the monoamines modulate the actions of the amino acid neurotransmitters. Their actions affect our brain much as a symphony conductor's actions spread to and affect many musicians and listeners. The interaction of a monoamine neurotransmitter with its postsynaptic receptor determines whether the message sent is excitatory or inhibitory.

Acetylcholine is distributed throughout our brain, especially in the centers controlling conscious movement (basal ganglia, motor cortex). It operates all voluntary muscles and many involuntary muscles, and it's the primary neurotransmitter for the parasympathetic nervous system (rest, recuperation). As many as 10 percent of our brain's synapses use acetylcholine, and its action is generally excitatory. It's also involved in learning and memory circuits. People with Alzheimer's disease suffer a depletion of neurons that process acetylcholine in the hippocampus.

Dopamine is synthesized in the substantia nigra in the basal ganglia (at the base of the cortex). It's sent into the limbic system and frontal lobe, where its neurons regulate complex emotional behaviors and conscious movements. Low levels of dopamine can result in Parkinson's disease, and high levels can result in schizophrenia.

Histamine operates in brain areas that regulate our emotions, and its circuitry is similar to that of norepinephrine. It is also involved in allergic conditions.

Norepinephrine (or noradrenalin) spreads to a very large number of connections throughout our brain from a very small brainstem structure called the locus coeruleus. It's the primary neurotransmitter for the sympathetic nervous system (arousal, activation, and flight-or-fight behaviors). *Epinephrine* (or adrenaline) is chemically and functionally related to norepinephrine.

Serotonin spreads throughout our brain from the raphe nucleus in the brainstem. Serotonin regulates body temperature, sensory perception, and the onset of sleep. Low serotonin levels appear to be a factor in the depression that accompanies seasonal affective disorder (SAD) and various aggressive behaviors.

Peptides

Some 50 peptides (or neuropeptides) have already been identified. They are chains of 2 to 39 amino acids that exert very powerful effects on complex behavior patterns, such as body fluid balance, sexual behavior, and pain or pleasure. Our brain and the peripheral nervous system contain many types of peptides, but each exists in very low concentration. Examples of types of peptides and some actions that have been associated with them follow:

- *Angiotensin II* triggers drinking behaviors.
- *Cholecystokinin* enhances the feeling of satiety after eating.
- *Endorphin, enkephalin,* and *dynorphin* are a class of opiate-related peptides that reduce intense pain and enhance euphoria.
- *Oxytocin* initiates uterine contractions in childbirth and lactation and enhances bonding between mother and child.
- *Somatostatin* inhibits intestinal secretion and regulates insulin secretion.
- *Substance P* transmits information on bodily pain to our brain.
- *Vasopressin* is involved in water retention, blood pressure, and memory.

Examples of How and Where Psychoactive Drugs Act in Neural Synaptic Areas

1. A drug can increase or decrease the amount of neurotransmitter released into the synapse: (a) Amphetamine and PCP (phencyclidine hydrochloride) increase the release of dopamine, (b) alcohol decreases the release of GABA (gamma-aminobutyric acid).

2. A drug can enhance the binding action of a neurotransmitter to its receptor: valium enhances the binding of GABA to its inhibitory receptors.

3. A drug's shape and electromagnetic properties can be so similar to a neurotransmitter's that the drug can mimic the neurotransmitter and its actions and effects: (a) opiates, such as heroin and morphine, mimic the endorphins, (b) mescaline and amphetamine mimic norepinephrine, (c) psychedelic drugs, such as LSD (lysergic acid diethylamide), mimic serotonin, (d) muscarine (obtained from a type of mushroom) and nicotine mimic acetylcholine, (e) alcohol and the barbiturates mimic GABA.

4. A drug can attach to a neurotransmitter receptor but not mimic the neurotransmitter's effects: (a) antipsychotic drugs, such as haloperidol, block dopamine receptors, (b) atropine and scopolamine block acetylcholine receptors.

5. A drug can block the neurotransmitter's re-uptake channels: (a) cocaine and amphetamine block dopamine and norepinephrine re-uptake channels (and so extend and intensify the action of the neurotransmitters until enzymes destroy the molecules), (b) tricyclic antidepressants block the re-uptake of norepinephrine and serotonin, (c) prozac blocks serotonin re-uptake channels.

6. A drug can inactivate enzymes that destroy neurotransmitters after their use in a synapse: antidepressants inactivate MAO (monoamine oxidase) enzymes that destroy monoamine neurotransmitters after they have acted on receptors.

7. A drug can modify second-messenger (cyclic AMP) effects and thus change a neuron's firing rate or metabolic activity: (a) Caffeine amplifies and extends the stimulant activity of cyclic AMP within a neuron, (b) lithium modulates extreme cyclic AMP effects.

APPENDIX B

A Brief Functional Explanation
of Neural Transmission

Neuron cell bodies and their many dendrite extensions constantly receive various levels of excitatory and inhibitory information from related neurons. This information is averaged within the cell body at the *axon hillock* (located where the axon leaves the cell body). Think of the axon hillock as fulfilling the thermostat function for a neuron. In a house, for instance, a thermostat maintains a comfortable heat level in a room by monitoring the heat level in the room and sending a message to the furnace when warm air is needed. But the temperature in a room differs in different places—perhaps 98.6 degrees on someone's face, 60 degrees on the window pane, and 150 degrees on the surface of a coffee cup. Such a system is designed so that a thermostat defines the room's temperature as whatever the temperature is at the thermostat's location. The axon hillock's monitoring system, however, is designed to average the various levels of information received.

If the average input at a given moment reaches the neuron's firing threshold, an *action potential* develops, and the message moves rapidly along the axon to the terminal. The movement of a neural message along an axon has been likened to an electrical charge. It does have some similarities, but neural messages don't move in the same way that electrical currents do. It is also more complicated biochemically than the following brief functional explanation, but you should be able to use this explanation in your work with students and colleagues.

The inside of an axon has a slight negative charge and the fluids outside the axon have a slight positive charge. When a neuron reaches its firing threshold, it propagates a signal down the axon that rapidly opens and closes a series of channels in the axon. When a set of channels opens, positively charged sodium ions from the fluids outside the neuron enter the axon. This action briefly changes the charge inside that part of the axon from negative to positive, and also triggers the opening of the next set of channels. The process is then repeated with the next set of channels. Think of a row of dominoes falling over. Each domino pushes the next one, just as each set of channels opens the next set.

After a set of channels opens, the sodium ions are pumped out, the channels close, and that part of the axon once again has a negative charge—until the next action potential propagates down the axon.

One type of glial cell wraps itself around long axons, creating a kind of insulating layer called myelin. This wrapping process reduces the number of functioning sodium channels along the axon, and so speeds up the message. Think of an unmyelinated axon as a slow local train (5 mph) that stops at every station, and a myelinated axon as a fast express train (200 mph) that stops infrequently.

When the axon's wave of permeability to sodium ions (the sequential opening and closing of channels) reaches the axon terminal, calcium ions enter the terminal, triggering the release of packets (vesicles) of neurotransmitters into the synapse, where they attach to the appropriate receptors on the dendrites and/or cell body of the postsynaptic neuron—and thereby pass their neuron's message to the next neuron.

INDEX